FIFTY-SEVEN
WORDS
THAT CHANGE THE
WORLD

FIFTY-SEVEN WORDS THAT CHANGE THE WORLD

A Journey Through the Lord's Prayer

DARRELL W. JOHNSON

REGENT COLLEGE PUBLISHING
Vancouver, British Columbia

Published 2005 by Regent College Publishing
5800 University Boulevard, Vancouver, BC V6T 2E4 Canada
Web: www.regentpublishing.com
E-mail: info@regentpublishing.com

Unless otherwise noted, Scripture quotations are from Today's
New International Version of the Bible, copyright © 2001,
2005 by the International Bible Society. Used by permission of
Zondervan Publishers.

Regent College Publishing is an imprint of the Regent
Bookstore <www.regentbookstore.com>. Views expressed in
works published by Regent College Publishing are those of the
author and do not necessarily represent the official position of
Regent College <www.regent-college.edu>.

Library and Archives Canada Cataloguing in Publication

Johnson, Darrell W., 1947-
Fifty-seven words that change the world: a journey
through the Lord's prayer / Darrell W. Johnson.

Includes bibliographical references.
ISBN 1-57383-278-2

1. Lord's prayer—Criticism, interpretation, etc. I. Title.

BV230.J54 2005   226.9'6077   C2004-903381-6

CONTENTS

ACKNOWLEDGEMENTS

B efore beginning our journey through the Lord's Prayer, I want to express my gratitude for the people with whom I have prayed and studied it. Thank you to the Sunday Morning Bible Study Class of St. John's Presbyterian Church of West Los Angeles, 1978; to the Young Adult Retreat of First Presbyterian Church of Colorado Springs, Colorado, 1981; to the Wednesday Morning Women's Bible Study Class of Union Church of Manila, Manila, Philippines, 1986; to the Tuesday Evening All-Church Bible Study of Fremont Presbyterian Church, Sacramento, California, 1991; to the Morning Seminar at Mount Hermon Christian Conference Center, Mount Hermon, California, 1991; to the Wednesday Evening Bible Study of Glendale Presbyterian Church, Glendale, California, 1998; to the students and faculty of Fuller Theological Seminary, All Seminary Day of Prayer, Pasadena, California, 1999; to the students and friends of Regent College, Day of Prayer, Vancouver, British Columbia, 2002; and to the congregation of First Baptist Church, Vancouver, British Columbia, who welcomed the preaching of the Prayer for the Sundays of the Fall of 2002 (the first time I actually preached the whole Prayer!).

I want to thank a number of people who helped me: my teaching assistant at Regent College, Margaret Carson, for turning my hard-to-read handwritten notes into perfectly legible type, and her husband Nathan who helped correct grammatical mistakes and looked for theological integrity; Michelle McFadden who, after leaving Regent, turned my instinctive oral style into words that speak from the page; and Marilyn Hoeppner of the Regent College staff who, in addition to everything else she does for us, graciously combed the final draft making sure you the reader can follow the flow of my thinking without awkward diversions. Any errors in the manuscript are, of course, fully my responsibility.

Finally, I want to thank my best friend and journey partner, my wife Sharon, for reading the entire manuscript a number of times and making helpful changes, for constantly encouraging me to go deeper in prayer, and for praying the Lord's Prayer for our children and me.

I dedicate these pages to my parents, Wally Johnson, now in heaven, and DeLores Johnson, still on earth. You were the first disciples to teach me to pray Jesus' Prayer. With you I long for that day when it is fully answered, and heaven and earth are one.

Our Father in heaven,
hallowed be your name,
your kingdom come,
your will be done,
on earth as it is in heaven.
Give us today our daily bread.
And forgive us our debts,
as we also have forgiven our debtors.
And lead us not into temptation,
but deliver us from the evil one.

Matthew 6:9-13

CHAPTER 1

BRINGING HEAVEN DOWN

J esus is brilliant. Yes, Jesus is good, and kind, and merciful, and strong. But the more I get to know Jesus, the more I am impressed by our Lord's sheer brilliance.

Nowhere is his brilliance more manifest than in the gift of the prayer he taught his disciples to pray, the prayer that has come to be known as "The Lord's Prayer." A mere fifty-seven words in the original Greek of Matthew's gospel, it manages to gather up all of life and brings it before God.

Have you ever observed that the only thing the first disciples of Jesus are recorded to have asked Jesus to teach them is, "Lord, teach us to pray"(Luke 11:1)? There is no record of anyone asking Jesus to teach them to lead, or to counsel, or to heal, or to cast out demons, or to preach. They may have asked him, but there is no record of them doing so. Why? Perhaps it is because they could see that Jesus' leading, counseling, healing, casting out, and preaching ministry emerged out of his relationship with his "Father." And they could see that the key to that relationship was prayer. Jesus, after all, was always slipping away to pray (Luke 5:16).

"Lord, teach us to pray." I understand the disciples' request to mean more than, "Jesus, teach us some new spiritual techniques that will help us stay awake when we pray and make us feel that our prayers matter." I take their request to mean, "Jesus, will you teach us how to relate to the one you call 'Father' the way you do?"

So Jesus teaches his disciples—and us—to pray fifty-seven words that are brilliant in their simplicity. These fifty-seven words change the way we understand God, ourselves, and the world. Indeed, they are fifty-seven words that, when prayed with even a modicum of faith, end up changing the world.

As is already clear, we are going to work with the version of the Prayer we find in Matthew 6 (fifty-seven words). We find a slightly different form in Luke 11:2-4 (thirty-eight words)—

> Father,
> hallowed be your name,
> your kingdom come.
> Give us each day our daily bread.
> Forgive us our sins,
> for we also forgive everyone who sins against us.
> And lead us not into temptation.

Jesus gives only five, not six petitions (no "your will be done") and where the last petition does not have the additional clause, "but deliver us from evil (or evil one)."

Why the difference? Probably because Jesus did not teach his "model prayer," as some call it, just once. He likely taught it many times in different settings with different groups of people, as a good teacher nuances a lesson for various settings.

We are going to work with Matthew's version because it is better known and more comprehensive. We will discover that the terms *name* and *kingdom* do not capture all that is involved in God's purposes in world.; that we also need to include *will*. And we are going to discover that "but deliver us from evil" is needed to rightly understand what "lead us not into temptation" means. We are also going to appreciate why the address "Father" needs to include "our" and "in heaven."

A WONDERFUL GIFT

The Lord's Prayer is one of the most wonderful gifts Jesus has given us. It is such a wonderful gift for at least three reasons.

First, the gift *frees us* from a universal anxiety of the human heart. It frees us from the anxiety about whether or not we are praying in a way that pleases the Living God. I hear that anxiety again and again, in my own soul and in the questions that people ask me as their pastor: "Am I getting it right?"; "Is what I'm praying acceptable to the Holy God?"

In the Lord's Prayer, Jesus, the Son of Mary, the Son of God, who has from all eternity lived in the heart of God the Father and comes from the heart of God the Father, tells us how to "get it right." "This, then, is how you should pray," he says (6:9), not implying that these are the only words to say, nor that this is the only order in which to say them, but rather offering us a model to help us enter into authentic communication with the Father. It is as though Jesus is saying in the Lord's Prayer, "Here then is the kind of praying that pleases my Father; this is the kind of praying the Father loves to hear and loves to answer."

Second, the Lord's Prayer is a wonderful gift because in it Jesus *reveals* the heart of the Living God. In the Lord's Prayer Jesus reveals what makes God's heart tick. It is as though Jesus is saying, "These are the concerns on my Father's heart." Jesus is revealing his understanding of what God is on about in the world, what God the Father is up to in your life and in my life, and in our neighbor's life. On his heart is the hallowing of his name, the coming of his kingdom, the fulfilling of his good pleasure, providing for us so we can live a kingdom life, canceling debts and reconciling us, protecting us from the attacks of Satan. There is only one place more revealing of the heart of God: John 17, where Jesus himself prays and we overhear him open his heart to his Father. As we pray the Lord's Prayer we are drawn deeper and deeper into the concern of the Triune God.

Third, the Lord's Prayer is such a wonderful gift because in it Jesus grants us what the mathematician-philosopher Blaise Pascal called "the dignity of causality."[1] When we pray, God is granting us the unspeakable privilege of partnering with him in fulfilling his purposes in the world. No prayer has given us that privilege more than the Lord's Prayer. As we pray the Prayer, we are joining the Living God in bringing about the realization of his heart's desire for the world.

This, by the way, is one of the major themes developed in the last book of the Bible, the book of Revelation. In chapters 6 through 8 we see Jesus Christ, the Lamb who was slain, breaking the seven seals of the scroll of history. As he does so, one seal at a time, we discover the secret of history the scroll contains. In each seal-scene *someone prays* to someone. Then comes the seventh seal. John writes, "And when he [the Lamb] opened the seventh seal, there was silence in heaven for about half an hour" (Rev 8:1).

Silence? But does not the worship scene in Revelation 4 show that "day and night" the heavenly creatures sing, "Holy, Holy, Holy"?

Yes, but then comes the seventh seal. The singing of "Holy, Holy, Holy" goes on day and night, and has gone on day and night since the creation of the world. Then it stops, and there is silence for half an hour.

Why the silence?

In John's vision an angel "who had a golden censer came and stood at the altar. He was given much incense to offer with the prayers of God's people on the golden altar before the throne. The smoke of the incense, together with the prayers of God's people, went up before God from the angel's hand" (8:3-4). And then all kinds of things begin to happen on the earth.

The point of this episode is that prayer, from the human side of things, moves history. The "movers and shakers" of history are those who pray. As the New Testament scholar George Beasley-Murray (an expert on the book of Revelation) commented:

> The significance of the picture can hardly be overestimated. No one was more aware than John of the limitations to what individual men and women can do to change the course of history and to bring in the kingdom of heaven, particularly in the face of the cosmic forces against them and the transcendent character of the kingdom itself.... But we can pray to him who has almighty power, and it would seem that God has willed that the prayers of his people should be part of the process by which the kingdom comes. The interaction between the sovereignty of God and the prayers of the saints is part of the ultimate mystery of existence. Faith is called on to take both seriously.[2]

"The dignity of causality." When we pray the Lord's Prayer we participate in the transformation of the world.

In this first chapter, I simply want to make five observations about the prayer as a whole. We should note first that the Prayer contains six requests or "petitions." In the subsequent chapters we will grapple with each of the six petitions one at a time. Each observation should stir our hearts and minds and make us want to go on to unwrap this wonderful gift Jesus has given us.

THE SCOPE OF THE PRAYER

First, we may observe the remarkable *scope* of the Prayer.[3] Jesus covers whatever it is we need to pray about. In these six short petitions he gathers up the whole of life.

The Lord's Prayer encompasses every dimension of our human existence. We are physical creatures so he teaches us to pray, "Give us this day our daily bread," and "your kingdom (of wholeness and health) come." We are relational creatures so he teaches us to pray, "Forgive us our debts as we have also forgiven our debtors." We are spiritual creatures so he teaches us to pray, "your name be hallowed," for we cannot live without knowing the name of him who made us, and "lead us not into temptation, but deliver us from the evil one."

Furthermore, the Lord's Prayer encompasses all of time: past, present, future. Our greatest need as we look to the past is forgiveness, so he teaches us to pray, "forgive us our debts as we forgive our debtors." Our greatest need as we look to the present is sustenance, so he teaches us to pray, "give us this day our daily bread." Our greatest need as we look to the future is guidance and protection from all that would threaten to undo us. So he teaches us to pray, "lead us not into temptation, but rescue us from the evil-one who seeks to destroy us."

Name any need, any concern, any longing, and it is covered by Jesus' Prayer. Nothing is left out. Nothing is too big. Nothing is too small. The German preacher and theologian Helmut Thielicke thus entitled his book *The Prayer that Spans the World*. Commenting on the scope of the Lord's Prayer, Thielicke writes that it covers "the world of everyday trifles and universal history, the world with its hours of joy and bottomless anguish, the world of citizens and soldiers, the world of monotonous routine and sudden terrible catastrophe, the world of carefree children and . . . of problems that can shatter grown men."[4]

Throughout church history pastors and theologians have spoken of the Lord's Prayer as "the sum of the Christian life." Everything we need to live the Christian life is embodied in the Prayer. It dawned on me a few of years ago that the Lord's Prayer also gives us a very helpful outline for discipling one another into maturity in Christ. We first learn God's name, God's character, who God is and what God is like. Then we begin to learn what his kingdom is all about, and how to live in it while living in the world. Then we begin to learn his will, his pleasures, his great purpose for his people and for the world, discovering how he wants us to cooperate with him as he fulfills his gracious plan. Then we learn to trust him for our bread, for our sustenance. We learn to take greater risks for him, as we can trust him more. Then we learn forgiveness; we begin to experience the grace and mercy of God that cancels all our debts, and which then frees us to extend mercy to others, even to our enemies. And then we begin to understand the nature of the spiritual battles in which humanity is caught; we learn how to stand against the onslaught of evil's temptations.

The scope of the Lord's Prayer is everything, every moment, every dimension of life. As the Czech scholar Jan Milic Lochman puts it, "The arc of the prayer spans the whole of cosmic reality with its heights and depth."[5]

THE FLOW OF THE PRAYER

Our Lord's Prayer can be divided into two halves—petitions one to three, and petitions four to six. The first half uses the pronoun *your*; the second half uses the pronoun *us*. Your name, your kingdom, your will. Give us our daily bread. Forgive us our debts. Lead us not into temptation. Deliver us. Jesus is teaching us to first and foremost begin praying God's agenda, not ours.

When many of us pray we begin with our needs: "Father, give me. . . ." There is nothing inherently wrong with that, but Jesus teaches us to begin, "Father, hallow your name, bring your kingdom, do your will." Why begin here? Because if we begin here, our agendas are then put into proper perspective. And, surprisingly, our needs do not then feel as "weighty." How often do we spend time praying only to emerge weary and overburdened? Could it be because we have not grasped what Jesus is telling us? If we begin with the Father's concerns, our concerns are put into his perspective.[6] Indeed, the more we pray the first half of the Prayer, the more we discover that our greatest needs are in fact being addressed. We discover that our real need is to see the Father's agenda fulfilled.

THE CENTER OF THE PRAYER

We should also note the *center* of Jesus' Prayer: the little clause "on earth as it is in heaven." The prepositional phrase goes with each of the first three petitions: your name be hallowed, *on earth as it is in heaven*; your kingdom come, *on earth as it is in heaven*; your will be done, *on earth as it is in heaven.* It is possible that the clause also goes with each of the second three petitions: give us this day our daily bread, *on earth as it is in heaven*; forgive us our debts as we forgive our debtors, *on earth as it is in heaven*; lead us not into temptation, but deliver us from the evil-one, *on earth as it is in heaven.*

The Lord's Prayer stands at the center of Jesus' Sermon on the Mount, in the collection of sayings where he describes what happens when the kingdom breaks in and takes hold of us. At the center of the Sermon on the Mount, in the Lord's Prayer, is the central clause: "on earth as it is in heaven." It captures the passion of the living God to bring the reality of heaven on earth. It is, after all, one of the reasons he became one of us.

In heaven, right now, the Father's name is being hallowed, his kingdom is being actualized, and his will is being done. *"O Father, make it so on earth!"* That is what Jesus is teaching us to pray. *"O Father, bring heaven down on earth right here!"*

To pray the Lord's Prayer is to participate in heaven's invasion of the earth. To pray the Lord's Prayer is to participate in a revolution of huge proportions. *"O Father, your name is hallowed in heaven; hallow it on earth, in me, in my family, in this city. O Father, your kingdom has come in heaven; cause it to come on earth, in my house, in my neighborhood, in this country. O Father, your will is done in heaven; make it be done on earth, in my work place, in the work places in Vancouver and Seattle and Dallas and Mexico City and Tokyo and Baghdad and Calcutta and Nairobi. O Father, your name be hallowed; your kingdom come, your will be done on Main Street and Wall Street, as it is in heaven!"* You can see then that to pray the Lord's Prayer is to engage in a cosmic act!

THE VERBS OF THE PRAYER

We do well to pay attention to the *verbs* of the Lord's Prayer. *Hallow, come, be done, give, forgive, lead not,* and *deliver.* These are all powerful verbs, all in the imperative mood. (So are the others, except "lead not" which is in the subjunctive.)

What is the imperative mood? Here is how one grammarian puts it: "The imperative is the mood of command or entreaty— the mood of volition. It is the genius of the imperative to express the will to will." The grammar goes on to say, "Normally the imperative carried with it a very forcible tone of command.

The ancient Greeks so regarded it, and hence never employed the imperative in communication with superiors."[7]

Surprisingly, the verbs of the Lord's Prayer, addressed to the Superior of superiors, *are in the imperative.* They are commands, not requests. Be hallowed! Be come! Be done! All in the command form. To pray the Lord's Prayer is to command—not to ask—but to command. Not that human beings are to order God around. Not at all! And yet, the verbs are in the imperative.

Now remember that it is Jesus himself who teaches us to do this. He is the one who put the verbs in the imperative. It is Jesus who is telling us to speak to the Father so boldly, so forcibly. He is the Son who knows the Father, who knows the Father's heart and mind. And he, the Son, the only-begotten Son, the Beloved Son with whom the Father is well pleased, tells us to say, "Be hallowed! Your name—Come! Your kingdom—Be done! Your will."

This may strike you as somewhat audacious. Who are we to speak to God in such a manner? What helps is to further know that the verbs in the first three petitions are in the passive voice.[8] "Be hallowed, come, be done." They are passive to introduce the note of reverence. It is too much to command and order the Father. The passive voice softens the tone. Instead of "do it," it is "be done." It is not as "in your face." Yet even that is bold enough.

But the verbs are passive for a more fundamental reason. *Only God can do what we are asking to have done.* Only God can hallow his name. Only God can bring his kingdom. Only God can do his will. The prayer is not what many believers have over the years thought it to be: the prayer is not, "let *us* hallow your name." The prayer is not, "let *us* bring in your kingdom." The prayer is not "let *us* do your will." The prayer is "Father, *you* do it! You hallow your name on earth as it is in heaven. You bring your kingdom on earth as it is in heaven. You make your will be done on earth as it is in heaven." Do you see the difference? It changes the whole tone of the prayer. We are asking God to do what only God can do. We are "commanding" that God do what only God can do. *We* might be involved; indeed, we *want* to be involved in the process of the kingdom coming, for instance. But *we* are not the ones making it come. As D. Elton Trueblood put it, "We mistake the kingdom request greatly if we think we are the chief actors in the drama. We may be needed, but the fundamental work for which we pray is God's work."[9] Professor Stendahl of Harvard University reminds us that the prayer "asks for the establishment of the kingdom of God, by God for us, not by us for God."[10] *Father, you do it, for only you can do it. You bring heaven down to earth.*

There is no doubt in my mind that the world is changed by standing up and preaching the Gospel. (That is why I have now given myself to teaching preaching at Regent College.) But the world is chiefly transformed by getting down on our knees and praying imperatives—"Do it, do it, do it." Or, more reverently, praying passive imperatives, "be done, be done, be done."

THE MECHANICS OF THE PRAYER

The Lord's Prayer *works* because of "Our Father who art in heaven." We often say, or hear said, "prayer works." That is only so because of the one to whom we pray *works*.

"Father." "In heaven." Both, not one without the other. "Father": the will to do what he is asked. "In heaven": the ability to do what he is asked.

As a young boy learning to pray I did not like the clause "in heaven" because it seemed to suggest that God was "way up there," or "way out there." It made me feel I as if I had to start the prayer shouting, "Father, far, far, away . . . can you hear me?" But that is not at all what the clause would suggest to a Jew

21

living in first-century Palestine. "In heaven" literally means "in the heavens," or "all around us."

In our culture we have come to think of heaven being "above us," but it also means "beneath us and alongside us." We are surrounded by the heavens.[11] The heavens are the atmosphere in which we live. We live in a multi-dimensional universe. Heaven is one of those dimensions, very close at hand. Jesus is praying "Father in the heavens"; "Father all around us"; and "Father very close at hand."

The clause "in heaven" would also conjure up in the minds of first-century Jews the idea of God on his throne. Earlier in Jesus' Sermon on the Mount, we read these words, "But I tell you, do not swear an oath at all: either by heaven, for it is God's throne; or by the earth, for it is his footstool" (Matt 5:34-35). "In heaven" means "on the throne." If this is not so, then we are wasting our breath praying the Lord's Prayer. Sure, it may be therapeutic to pray, but if the one to whom we pray is not on the throne, then we have no real hope that he can do what we ask him to do. At best he can say, "I am doing my best." Jesus is telling us that there is a throne—all around us—and someone is sitting on it. We can, therefore, dare to hope that when we pray something happens.

"Our Father." This, finally, is the reason praying the Lord's Prayer "works." On the throne of the universe is a Father. Yes, on the throne is a Creator, a mighty Creator. And yes, on the throne is a Sovereign Master, the Rock of Ages. But what Jesus emphasizes again and again is that on the throne is a Father—*his* Father. The Father *he* knows and loves and trusts.

"Father" is a problematic image for many people in our day, and not only for women. Many men also struggle with calling God "Father." The word "Father" is fraught with feelings of disappointment, pain, anger, in some cases, an awful sense of abandonment.

A number of years ago I was wrestling with this. I said to Jesus, *"I like your prayer, but it would be so much more inviting for more people if you had taught us to pray the prayer to you. Where are you in this prayer?"* And in my mind I heard John 14:9, "Anyone who has seen me has seen the Father." I sensed Jesus saying to me, "The Father is just like me." The Father, God the Father, is just as good, just as gentle, just as kind, just as approachable, just as vulnerable, just as welcoming, just as generous as Jesus. Jesus' open arms are the open arms of his Father. Jesus' open heart is the open heart of his Father. It is the passion of Jesus to help us know his Father *as* he knows him, to love his Father *as* he loves him, to trust his Father *as* he trusts him.

The folks in the Alcoholics Anonymous recovery groups say, in step three, "We entrusted ourselves to God as we understood God." That troubled me for a long time until on a recent plane flight I was reading a book by business leader Howard Butt, Jr., who makes the simple observation that the "only way any of us ever prays to God is as we understand him."[12] That is just the way it is. All of our understanding of God is shaped by our experience of earthly fathers and mothers. But Jesus comes to us, and calls us to *follow him into his understanding of "Father."* His goal is to correct our understanding of "Father"; to replace our misguided concepts associated with the word with his. And to make **this** happen, he breathes his Holy Spirit into our hearts, who enables us to cry out the way he does, "Abba, Father" (Rom 8:15-16; Gal 4:4-7). Jesus brings us into his experience of the Father.

On the throne is the Father of the Lord Jesus Christ, who, because of what he has done in Jesus is our Father, too. "Who," says Jesus, "knows what you need before you ask him" (Matt 6:8). Good news! Why? Because we do not know what we need. We *think* we know. We think we see the whole picture. We think we recognize all the factors involved in our circumstances. We think we understand ourselves, our desires, our longings, our fears. We do not. But our Father does.[13]

Do you see what this does for us? It frees us from having to have everything figured out before and while we pray. It frees us from having to have the right words. "Just come," Jesus is saying, "say what is on your hearts the most honest way you can. The Father knows what you need."

"Thank God," wrote Helmut Thielicke, "that our prayer does not depend on our expressing the correct desires, that it does not depend on our making a correct 'diagnosis' of our needs and troubles and then presenting God with a properly phrased and clearly outlined prayer-proposition."[14] The Father knows our needs *beyond* the expressed needs. He knows our needs *contrary* to the expressed needs.

The Father of Jesus, who by grace is *our* Father, knows we need bread, sustenance, forgiveness, reconciliation, guidance and protection. He knows we need to experience his name being hallowed, and his kingdom coming, and his will being done. It turns out that our greatest need is the Father himself.

The scope of the prayer is every moment, every issue. The flow of the prayer is your, your, your, us, us, us. The center of the prayer is "on earth as it is in heaven." The verbs of the prayer are bold and forceful: "Be!" And the reason the prayer works? "Our Father in heaven." The Father Jesus knows, the Father Jesus loves, the Father Jesus trusts, is the Father who sits on the throne.

That is why praying the Lord's Prayer, and praying it with our whole lives, changes the world.

PRACTICING THE PRAYER

At the front of this book are seven lines: the opening line of the Lord's Prayer and each of the six petitions. New Testament scholar N. T. Wright has suggested a helpful way to implement what we have learned so far: pray one line a day for the coming week. "The 'prayer of the day,'" he says, "then becomes the lens through which you see the world."[15] So on Sunday, pray "Our Father in heaven." On Monday pray, "Hallowed be your name, on earth as it is in heaven," joining others all over the world who are asking God to make his name known and honored. On Tuesday pray, "Your kingdom come, on earth as it is in heaven," joining others across the face of the globe who are also asking God to cause his kingdom to break in. And so on up to Saturday, when we will be asking God to protect us and our fellow-citizens from the machinations of the evil-one. Each day of the week we can join the Father's Son and multitudes of his brothers and sisters in the cosmic act of bringing heaven down.

CHAPTER 2

MAKE YOURSELF REAL

Our Father in heaven,
hallowed be your name, on earth as it is in heaven.

Why does Jesus teach us to begin here? Given that the dominant note of his own teaching and preaching is the kingdom of God, why not begin there? "Our Father in heaven, your kingdom come." We can connect with that prayer relatively quickly, even if we have mistaken ideas about the nature of God's kingdom. But "Father, hallowed be your name"?

The first petition of the Lord's Prayer is for most of us the most difficult petition to get our minds around. Jan Milic Lochman asks the question for us: "What are we to make of the abstract sounding words like 'name' and 'hallowed' in the secularized world of today? . . . . To be sure, one might put the same question regarding the other petitions, but here at the outset the lack of relevance seems particularly great and therefore the chance of understanding particularly small as compared to what follows."[1]

"Our Father in heaven, hallowed be your name, on earth as it is in heaven."

As abstract sounding as it is, it turns out that this is precisely where we ought to begin, for this is where Jesus himself begins and ends. Jesus teaches us to pray this petition first because this is what he prays first, and second and third, and fourth and fifth! I will put it more boldly: at the center of Jesus' being, at the center of Jesus' identity and mission is his passion for his Father's name being hallowed.

How do I know that? Because of the *other* Lord's Prayer, the prayer Jesus prayed recorded in the seventeenth chapter of the Gospel according to John. It was on the night Jesus was handed over to death. John writes, "And lifting up his eyes to heaven, Jesus said, 'Father, the hour has come; glorify your Son, that your Son may glorify you'"(17:1). He goes on, "I glorified you on the earth, having accomplished the work you gave me to do" (17:4). And what is that work? "I manifested your name to those you gave me out of the world . . . I have made your name known" (17:6). "While I was with them, I was keeping them in your name which you have given me" (17:12). "Righteous Father, though the world does not know you, I know you, and they know that you have sent me. I have made you known to them, and will continue to make you known in order that the love you have for me may be in them and I myself may be in them" (17:25-26).

Jesus teaches us to pray, "Father, hallowed be your name," because that is what *he* prays. That is what *he* lives and dies to see happen "on earth as it is in heaven." Yes, Jesus lives and dies to see the kingdom of God come; which is why the kingdom is such a dominant note of his teaching and preaching. Yes, he lives and dies to see the will of God be done; which is why Jesus agonizes in the Garden of Gethsemane, "Not my will, but yours be done," and why in the book of Hebrews Jesus quotes the line from the Psalms, "I have come to do your will, my God" (Heb 10:7; Ps 40:7-8). From first to last, and at every point in between, Jesus lives and dies to see the Father's name be hallowed on earth as it is in heaven.

WHAT'S IN A NAME?

So what is Jesus getting at when he uses the word *name*? In the biblical world, names were more than mere labels. Not only did they describe realities, they partook of—perhaps even shaped—the realities to which they referred. That is why it was so important in biblical times to know a person's name. A name often stood for "the personal and incommunicable character" of a person.[2]

Nabal, for instance, means "fool"; if you read his story in 1 Samuel you see how magnificently he lives out his name. Isaac means "laughter"; if you read his story in Genesis you find yourself entering into the delight his parents had in his miraculous birth. Peter means "rock"; when you read his story in the Gospel you enter into the process by which shifting sand is transformed into solid rock.

To speak of someone's "name" in this sense is a way of refering to their "character," "personality," or "reputation." To know the name of a human being is to know some essential truth about the person's character. To put it in modern terms, a name gives us "a mini personality profile." It is easy for us to underestimate the signifance of such a profile. We live in a age of police checks and credit ratings. Those living in biblical times did not. They could only go on the basis of the name. No wonder Proverbs tells us that a "good name is more desirable than great riches; to be esteemed is better than silver or gold" (22:1).

To know the name of God is to know some essential truth about God's character. "God" is not God's name. "God" is a descriptive word, not a name. God has a name, a personal name, a first name, and many nicknames.

"Father in heaven, hallowed be your character, your personality, on earth as it is in heaven."

THE MEANING OF "HALLOWED"

Now the more difficult word, "hallowed." What is Jesus getting at when he uses the verb *hallow*? Literally, it means "to holy-fy." The verb is related to the adjective "holy." "Your name be holy-fied." It is the same word translated "sanctify" in other biblical texts. Jesus uses the word in his prayer recorded in John 17. "Sanctify them by the truth. . . For them I sanctify myself, that they too may also be truly sanctified" (John 17:17-19). This verse could also be translated "hallow them by the truth . . . for them I hallow myself, that they may also be truly hallowed." Sanctify means "to make holy." "Be-made-holy your name."

God is already holy. God's name, the Father's name, is already holy. So in the first petition the verb means, "Your name be treated as holy." That is, "your name be treated as infinitely precious, your name be highly valued, above all other values." Thus this verb has the sense of praise, honor, exalt, magnify, revere, glorify.[3]

None of this can happen unless and until God's name is known. So "hallowed" has the deeper meaning of being revealed, manifest, made known, or best of all, made *real*. "Your name, so infinitely precious, be made known on earth as you are in heaven." "Your name, so greatly to be valued because it is you yourself, be made real on earth as it is in heaven."

We hear and see these nuances of the words "name" and "hallowed" throughout the Bible. "LORD, our Lord, how majestic is your name in all the earth! You have set your glory above the heavens" (Ps 8:1). "Save me, O God, by your name; vindicate me by your might" (Ps 54:1). "Praise the LORD! Praise the LORD, you his servants; praise the name of the LORD. Let the name of the LORD be praised, both now and forevermore. From the rising of the sun to the place where it sets, the name of the LORD is to be praised" (Ps 113:1-3).

"Let them praise the name of the LORD, for his name alone is exalted; his glory is above heaven and earth." "Glorify the LORD with me; let us exalt his name [his character, his personality] together" (Ps 34:3). "Do not profane my holy name, for I must be acknowledged as holy by the Israelites; I am the LORD who made you holy" (Lev 22:32).

And the prophet Isaiah, speaking of the events of the Exodus when God brought his people out of Egypt, asks

Who sent his glorious arm of power
to be at Moses' right hand,
who divided the waters before them,
to gain for himself everlasting renown,
who led them through the depths?
Like a horse in open country,
they did not stumble;
like cattle that go down to the plain,
they were given rest by the Spirit of the LORD.
This is how you guided your people
to make for yourself a glorious name. (Isaiah 63:12-14)

So pull it all together. "Father in heaven, hallowed be your name, on earth as it is in heaven." "Name" equals character, attributes, personality, glory, fame, reputation. *Name* means who God is and what God is like. "Hallowed": holy-fy, treat as holy, honor, exalt, magnify, glorify. Hallowed means reveal, manifest, make known, make real. Thus we might pray, *"Father in heaven—Father of our Lord Jesus, our own Father—make real your character and magnify your name on earth as it is in heaven. Father, make yourself real on earth as you are real in heaven; enhance your reputation in all the earth."*

Can you think of any more appropriate way to begin to pray?

Now, remember from the introductory chapter: the first petition is not "let *us* hallow your name." That is an appropriate prayer to pray, and it turns out that we get to be part of God's answering the first petition. But the prayer here is not, "let *us* hallow your name." It is not even "give us power to hallow your name." The first petition of the Lord's Prayer can be paraphrased, "You, Father, hallow your name." Jesus is teaching us to ask the Father to do what only the Father can do. "Father, you honor your name, you magnify your character, you manifest your personality, you make yourself real on earth as it is in heaven, you enhance your reputation in all the universe. Yes, we will gladly be part of the process. But we cannot make it happen. *Only you* can display the glory of who you are. O Father, you do it!"

And from the throne we hear, "I will hallow my name!" Repeatedly we hear God express this resolve. "Do not worship any other god, for the LORD, whose name is Jealous, is a jealous God" (Exod 34:14). God values his name, his character, his personality, and does everything possible to make sure it is known and revered and understood and loved. "And I will be zealous for my holy name" (Ezek 39:25). The living God always speaks and acts in ways that honor his name. How many times do we hear the phrase, "for my name's sake" or "for his name's sake"?

"For the sake of his great name the LORD will not reject his people, because the LORD was pleased to make you his own"

(1 Sam 12:22). "He refreshes my soul. He guides me along the right paths for his name's sake" (Ps 23:3). He has revealed himself as the restorer and guider, and will always act in ways consistent with that revelation.

"For the sake of your name, LORD, forgive my iniquity, though it is great" (Ps 25:11). He has revealed himself as the one who forgives anyone who comes in repentance, and will always act in ways consistent with that revelation. The apostle John says in his first letter, "Your sins have been forgiven on account of his name" (1 John 2:12). The Psalmist writes, "Since you are my rock and my fortress, for the sake of your name lead me and guide me" (Ps 31:3). "Help us, God our Savior, for the glory of your name; deliver us and forgive our sins, for your name's sake" (Ps 79:9). The prophet Jeremiah cries out to God on the basis of his name. "Although our sins testify against us, do something, LORD, for the sake of your name!" (Jer 14:7). "You are among us, LORD, and we bear your name; do not forsake us!" (Jer 14:9).

In the book of Ezekiel we encounter one of the most revealing texts of Scripture. God, speaking to the captive Jews in Babylon, tells his people that he is ready to save them:

> Therefore say to the house of Israel, "This is what the Sovereign LORD says: It is not for your sake, house of Israel, that I am going to do these things, but for the sake of my holy name, which you have profaned among the nations where you have gone. I will show the holiness of my great name, which has been profaned among the nations, the name you have profaned among them. Then the nations will know that I am the LORD, declares the Sovereign LORD, when I am proved holy through you before their eyes." (Ezekiel 36:22-23)

Do you see now why the first petition of the Lord's Prayer is the first? Jesus is inviting us to enter into the deepest passion of God's heart; "Father, hallow your name."

Is there a way to enter into this seemingly abstract prayer more concretely? Yes. We can "pray back." Not "pay back." That is simply not possible. But we *can* "pray back." The Living God has revealed who he is and what he is like. We enter into the first petition of the Lord's Prayer by "praying back" God's self-revelation. God has made himself known in a number of names and titles. We simply "pray back" those names and titles. God has made himself known in a number of events. We simply "pray back" what is made real in those events.

PRAYING BACK THE NAMES OF GOD

God has manifested his character as *El Shaddai*—the mighty God, *El Roi*—the God who sees, *El Rophe*—the God who heals. It is good for us to pray the names back. *"O Father, you are* El Shaddai, *the Mighty One. Make yourself real as the Mighty One in my life as it is in heaven; enhance your reputation as the Mighty One in my life as it is in heaven."*

God is *Adonai,* our Master. And he's our Rock. And Fortress. And Refuge. And Holy One. And Cleansing Fire. *"O Father, make yourself real to me as Cleansing Fire; enhance your reputation as Cleansing Fire in this place."*

God is the Fountain of living water, the Lover of our soul, the Shepherd of the flock. *"O Father, my neighbors are having a hard time. Please make yourself real to them as the Shepherd who carries his sheep; enhance your reputation as the Good Shepherd in my apartment building."*

This is what I mean by "praying back" the character of God revealed in his names.

The name above every name—God's covenant name—is Yahweh. Many English-speakers are familar with this name of God being rendered "Jehovah." But the general consensus among biblical scholars today is that Yahweh is probably the closest equivalent to the original pronunciation. The name is rendered by most English versions of the Bible as LORD, using capital letters. God meets Moses out in the desert, in a bush on fire but not being consumed. "What is your name?" Moses asks. God replies, "I AM WHO I AM. Say to the children of Israel, I AM has sent me to you" (Exod 3:14). Then he instructs Moses:

> "Say to the Israelites, 'The LORD, the God of your fathers—the God of Abraham, the God of Isaac and the God of Jacob—has sent me to you.'
> "This is my name forever,
> the name you shall call me
> from generation to generation." (Exodus 3:15)

Yahweh means "I AM," but not just in the philosophical sense of "I exist." It also means "I AM" in a relational sense: "I AM there with you and for you." Yahweh is the covenant name. All the covenants God has ever made with humanity have the phrase, "I, Yahweh, will be your God." Meaning, "I will be your God with you and for you." Meaning, "All that makes me be God I place at your disposal." Meaning, "All that I am I give to you."

Pray it back: *Father, Yahweh, manifest all that your name means in my life and the life of those I know, as it is in heaven. Enhance your reputation as the God who is with us and for us.* Take any one of the names or titles for God and pray it back.

PRAYING BACK GOD'S REVELATION

The Living God has also manifested his character in actions, in concrete historical events. Therefore we can also pray the revelation back. At the beginning God manifested himself as Creator, as the one who simply speaks into the emptiness and chaos, and brings the universe into being. *"Father, there is so much emptiness in our time. We are seemingly on the verge of chaos. Reveal yourself as the God who brings fullness and order; enhance your reputation as the one who brings life out of nothing."* God revealed himself in the call to Abraham and Sarah to leave their home, calling them out of the land of Ur (what is now Iraq) to become a blessing to all nations. Pray it back. *"Father, in our time, reveal yourself as the one who blesses Israel so Israel can bless Iraq."* God reveals himself in the Exodus, acting to free slaves from captivity without the slaves needing to take up arms. *"Father, all over the world people are caught in all kinds of oppression; manifest yourself as the God who comes to set the captives free!"* Later on Moses cries out, "Show me your glory!" "Let me see you in all your glory." God responds, "You cannot see my face," at least not yet, but "I will proclaim my name, the LORD, in your presence." So Moses hides in the cleft of a rock. And God passes by, and says, "Yahweh, Yahweh God, the compassionate and gracious God, slow to anger, abounding in love and faithfulness" (Exod 34:6-7). Pray the revelation back: *"Father, show yourself in my work-place as compassionate and gracious; enhance your reputation in my office as slow to anger and abounding in mercy."* At the burning bush God says to Moses, "I have indeed seen the misery of my people in Egypt. I have heard them crying out . . . and I am concerned about their suffering. So I have come down to rescue them" (Exod 3:7-8). Pray the revelation back: *"Father, manifest yourself in our time as the God who sees our suffering, who hears our cries, who feels our pain; enhance your name as the God who therefore comes down."*

He does, and has, come down, in the incarnation. In Jesus of Nazareth, God became (and remains) one of us. Jesus' name in Hebrew is Joshua, or Y'shua. It means "Yahweh saves," or "Yahweh to the rescue." In every word Jesus speaks, in every deed Jesus does, the nature and character of the saving God is being revealed. Pray the events of Jesus' life back to God: *"You welcomed outcasts, you healed the sick, you reconciled the estranged. O Father, make real all of this now in our century as you did in the first century. Enhance your reputation as the God who puts broken people back together again."*

The religious leaders of the day did not like everything that was being manifested. They especially did not like the fact that Jesus was hanging around with the wrong kind of people. "This man welcomes sinners and eats with them," they say in disgust. Jesus then teaches them the parables of Luke 15, the parables of the shepherd who goes looking for his lost sheep, the woman who goes looking for her lost coin, and the father who reaches out to his lost sons.

Pray it back: *"O Father, make real in our city your love for sinners; enhance your reputation in this church as the God who welcomes sinners and eats with them."*

And then come the events of Holy week, the events of Palm Sunday, Good Friday, Easter. On Palm Sunday Jesus rides into the city of Jerusalem. Some Greeks come seeking Jesus. Jesus answers, "The hour has come, Father, glorify your name!" John 12:28, "Father, glorify your name!" "Father, magnify your character, honor your reputation." And John says a voice from heaven came saying, "I have glorified it, and will glorify it again" (12:28). "I have and I will."

"I have"—how? In the works of Jesus which he has already done. In turning water into wine; in giving sight to the blind; in multiplying five loaves of bread and two fish to feed over 5,000 people; in raising Lazarus form the dead. "I have glorified my name."

"And I will"—how? In the events about to unfold, in the events of Holy Week. "The hour has come." Trace the word "hour" through the Gospel of John and you will see that it always points to Jesus' death. The "hour" involves Jesus being seized by people who want to destroy him. "The hour has come, Father. The hour for me to glorify your name has finally come."

Jesus says, "Unless a kernel of wheat falls to the ground and dies, it remains only a single seed; but if it dies it produces many seeds" (John 12:24). What is this? What does falling into the earth and dying have to do with hallowing the name of the Father?

Everything! The dying of Jesus on the cross is the final glorification of the name of God! Jesus' death on the cross, his handing himself over to the ones who want to destroy him, is the great moment when the nature and character of the Living God is finally and decisively manifested and honored.

John Calvin writes:

> For in the cross of Christ, as in a splendid theatre, the incomparable goodness of God is set before the whole world. The glory of God shines, indeed, in all creatures, on high and below, but never more brightly than in the cross . . . .
>
> If it be objected that nothing could be less glorious than Christ's death . . . , I reply that in that death we see a boundless glory which is concealed from the ungodly.[4]

A grain of wheat only lives if it dies. It fulfills its reason for being as it gives itself away in death. Indeed, if it does not die, it does not live; it merely exists alone, unfilled. "Now is my soul troubled," says Jesus. "And what shall I say? 'Father, save me from this hour?' No, it is for this very reason I came to this hour. Father, glorify your name!" (12:27-28). That is the deepest passion of Jesus' being: to reveal the nature and character of his Father. The great moment of glorification finally comes, and Jesus speaks of falling and dying as a grain of wheat! Why? Because in giving his life for the world, in emptying himself in servant love, the nature and character of God is fully manifested for the entire world to see.

Pray the moment back. *"O Father, make all this real in my life; enhance your reputation as the self-emptying Servant God on earth as it is in heaven."*

It's not too hard to see why the first petition is first. Jesus is teaching us to begin by allowing God to be God. *"O Father, be all that you are on earth that you are in heaven."*

And the Father answers by pointing us to his Son, Emmanuel, "God with us" (Matt 1:23). It turns out that the one who teaches us to pray so boldly is himself the answer to the prayer. In *Jesus* the Father's name is finally and fully hallowed.

3

RULE WITHOUT RIVAL

Our Father in heaven, your kingdom come,
on earth as it is in heaven.

It has rightly been said that this petition ought to have come with a warning label. In an oft-quoted passage, Annie Dillard reminds us of how flippantly we often treat such prayer:

> Does anyone have the foggiest idea what sort of power we so blithely invoke? Or, as I suspect, does no one believe a word of it? The churches are children playing on the floor with their chemistry sets, mixing up a batch of TNT to kill a Sunday morning. It is madness to wear ladies' straw hats and velvet hats to church; we should all be wearing crash helmets. Ushers should issue life preservers and signal flares; they should lash us to our pews.[1]

This second petition of the Lord's Prayer began to *explode* in me during the first of the four years my family lived in the Philippines. During Fall of 1985 and the Winter of 1986 you could feel the tension everywhere. Ferdinand Marcos, the corrupt dictator, was tightening his grip on the country. People who spoke out against his unjust ways were "disappearing," some were discovered murdered. All over the city of Manila believers were praying, "Your kingdom come!" with a great sense of urgency. Then, in February of 1986, we witnessed the so-called "People-Power Revolution." I say so-called because it should have been called "Praying-People-Power Revolution." We witnessed a "regime change" take place without anyone needing to resort to military intervention. I learned that year that to pray the second petition of the Lord's Prayer, "Your kingdom come on earth as it is in heaven," is one of, if not *the* most radical things a human being can do, for it turns out that in this petition we are asking God to bring about the most massive revolution imaginable.

In order to appreciate what it is Jesus is calling us to do in this prayer, we need to be reminded of the staggering *claim* Jesus made in his first sermon. But in order to appreciate that staggering claim we need to be reminded of the Jews' *concept* of history.

GOD AND HISTORY

In contrast to other people groups in Jesus' day, and in contrast to many people groups in our day, the Jews held a unique perspective on the movement of time and history. In the Hebrew view of things, history has purpose. It is moving toward a goal. Time is linear, history moves forward. Other worldviews see history as a series of chance, accidental events leading who knows where. History had no purposeful beginning, will have no purposeful end, and therefore has no purposeful middle. Still other worldviews see history as the endless repetition of the same cycle: spring, summer, fall, winter, spring, summer, fall, winter. Over and over. The goal of human existence is to get in sync with that endless rhythm, that cycle of birth, life, death, re-birth, life, death, re-birth, life, death and so on. Not so for the Hebrews. History is moving forward—maybe not in a straight line—but forward nonetheless, toward a meaningful goal. In spite of what felt like confusion and even madness, the Hebrews believed that the Living God is active in history, and is moving history toward its appointed end. That end is the kingdom of God.

This unique view of history is reflected in a Jewish prayer, which is similar to what Jesus teaches us to pray. In the Aramaic *Kaddish* we find, "May God let his kingdom rule in your lifetime and in your days and in the lifetime of the whole house of Israel, speedily and soon."[2]

In using the term "kingdom of God," the Hebrew writers of Scripture were not thinking of a place over which God would rule, nor even of an identifiable people over whom God would rule. Rather, "kingdom of God" or "kingdom of heaven" is a way of saying "God is acting as King." The kingdom of God refers to the dynamic reality of God acting as the King. The Hebrew prophets longed for the day when God would finally impose and establish his kingly-rule over the entire world. They longed for the day when God would intervene once and for all, and rule without rival. In the minds of the Jewish prophets this reign of God would be ushered in by God's messiah ("anointed one") on the so-called "Day of the Lord," the great and awesome Day. The period of time preceding the "Day of the Lord" was called the "end times." On that "Day" the Living God, "the Father who is in heaven," would intervene in history in a radical way and completely transform the broken world. God would come to *reverse* the effects of the fall of humanity.

On that "Day" God would judge human wickedness and wipe away all evil. God would vindicate those who dared to trust and obey in the face of the unbelief and disobedience of the kingdoms of this world. God would forgive repentant people and fill them with the Holy Spirit. On that "Day" God would rid creation of disease and pain and war and tears and death. On that "Day" God would destroy the evil one. The term "kingdom of God," therefore, refers to a brand new world order, centered in God's Messiah, in which human beings are re-made into the image of God and all of creation *restored* to God's original design.

THE KINGDOM AT HAND

"Pray then in this way," says Jesus, "your kingdom come, on earth as it is in heaven." Do you see what Jesus is encouraging us to ask God to do? "O God, hasten the coming of the Day of the Lord when your kingdom will be present in all its fullness." Hasten the Day of reversal and restoration! Hasten the Day of the new creation!

We mere human beings are given the privilege of inviting in God's glorious future. We are given the privilege of asking heaven to invade and occupy the earth. As amazing as that is, it does not exhaust the meaning of this prayer, for Jesus taught the prayer in the context of the staggering claim he made in his first public sermon.

The essence of his sermon is recorded in Mark 1:15. Jesus says, "The time is fulfilled, and the kingdom of God is at hand" (NASB).

"The time is fulfilled." The Greek word for "time" used here is *kairos*. The more usual word is the word *kronos*, from which we get our word "chronological." As my uncle, Dr. Emmett Johnson, used to put it, *kronos* is "tick-tock" time, time measured by clocks and calendars. *Kairos* time cannot be so measured. It is "opportunity time." *Kairos* time is that unique moment determined by God for the fulfillment of his divine purposes.

Let it astonish you afresh: Jesus came on the scene and the first thing he says is that "the time is fulfilled"—the *kairos* is now! He did not proclaim, "The Day of the Lord has arrived." The "Day" is still to come. What Jesus claimed was that in him the unique moment for the fulfillment of promise has *begun*: because of Jesus every day potentially participates in the *kairos*. Since the first Christmas Eve we are living in "fulfillment time," or as the Apostle Paul puts it, "in the fullness of time" (Gal 4:4, NASB).[3]

Every *kronos* moment can be a *kairos* moment. *Kairos* for what? Time for what? For the in-breaking of the kingdom! "The time is fulfilled," and what does Jesus claim next? "The kingdom of God is at hand." That is the good news, the gospel that Jesus preached and calls us to believe: in him and because of him the long awaited kingdom is at hand. It is in light of this "at-hand-ness" that he teaches us to pray, "your kingdom come."

So we need to ask what Jesus does mean by the term "at hand"? The term "at hand" literally means, "come near." Jesus means that the kingdom of God, the reign of God, God's new world order, has "come near." Does Jesus mean it is just about to arrive, so we should get ready? Or does he mean it is here—so we should grab hold and enter in? As you can imagine there is considerable scholarly debate on this issue and people want to settle on one or the other side of the issue. I believe, following many scholars from the full range of theological traditions, that taken in light of the whole New Testament, the term "at hand" is used in both senses—both "just about to arrive," and "right here, now." Jesus is announcing that in him and because of him the future reign of God spoken of by the prophets, the glorious new order of life, is both "just about to dawn on the world" and "is dawning right now."

Thus, after freeing a man from demon possession, Jesus says to the Pharisees: "If it is by the Spirit of God that I drive out demons, then the kingdom of God has come upon you" (Matt 12:28). The kingdom has come!

On another occasion Jesus said, "The Law and the Prophets were proclaimed until John [the Baptist]. Since that time, the good news of the kingdom of God is being preached" (Luke 16:16). Mortimer Arias of Bolivia can therefore write:

> Jesus was baptized by John, and John's disciples became the first disciples of Jesus. But between the two the threshold of the centuries has been crossed. John represented the end of one era—*before* the kingdom—and Jesus the beginning of another, the era *of* the kingdom, the "year of the Lord's reign."[4] (emphasis mine)

Jesus came into Galilee proclaiming, "the presence of the future."[5] In Jesus, "the time before the kingdom is finished, the time of the kingdom has begun."[6]

This is why after recording Jesus' staggering claim, the Gospel writers go on to record a series of Jesus' mighty deeds. Jesus' deeds validate Jesus' claim. Jesus' miracles demonstrate that indeed the future is breaking into the present, but they do more than validate the claim. They give us a picture of what God's kingdom is all about.[7] Jesus gives sight to the blind—that is the kingdom of God come near. Jesus causes the lame to walk—that is the Kingdom of God come near. Jesus touches and cleanses lepers—that is the kingdom of God come near. Jesus liberates those held captive by demonic powers—that is the kingdom, that is the new order, breaking into the present. Jesus heals the sick—that is the kingdom of God. Jesus befriends prostitutes and one of them comes and washes his feet with her tears—that is the kingdom. Jesus calms the wind and waves—that is the kingdom. Jesus multiplies the loaves to feed the hungry—that is the kingdom. Jesus champions the powerless; he stands in solidarity with the poor—that is the kingdom, that is God's new world order.

Jesus unites people the world divides. In his company are Simon the Zealot and Matthew the tax collector, two arch enemies. One represents an oppressive foreign government; the other, revolutionary insurgency—he's a terrorist. But in Jesus they become brothers! That is the kingdom of God come near.

Jesus calls women into his company, granting them dignity, and entrusting them with his gospel message. That is the reign of God, the new world order breaking into the present. Jesus has dinner with Zacchaeus, the corrupt tax collector. After the meal, Zacchaeus denounces his corrupt practices and offers to pay back four-fold those he had cheated. That is the kingdom of God come near. "Today salvation has come to this house," says Jesus (Luke 19:1-10).

Jesus fills ordinary people with the Holy Spirit; that is the kingdom, the blessing of the future breaking into the present. Jesus raises from the dead the daughter of Jairus, and a widow's son, and Lazarus. That is the kingdom of God! Jesus triumphs over the grave, he is resurrected! That is the reign of God, the new order of existence, breaking into the present from the future. Isn't this exciting?

Yet, a number of times in the Gospels we hear Jesus speaking of the kingdom as still to come. In the upper room, during the first Lord's Supper, Jesus says to the disciples, "I tell you I will not drink again of the fruit of the vine until the kingdom of God comes" (Luke 22:18). Until the kingdom comes. It was during the week before that night that Jesus taught the parables of waiting and watching. These parables call us to look forward to the coming reign of God. Jesus' basic exhortation in each of them is, "Be on the alert!" (Mark 13:37, NASB).

What is going on here? We are faced with the tension we encounter again and again in the New Testament, the tension in which the church must live and serve and pray. The tension is expressed in the phrase, "already, not-yet." In Jesus this glorious, redeeming, recreating reign of God is "already, not-yet." In Jesus God's new world order is already present in some form, but not-yet present in the form it will be on the Day of the Lord.

THE KINGDOM TO COME

Now we are getting to the heart of the second petition. What is the nature of this "already, not-yet?" It seems that the "already, not-yet" means "partial" versus "complete."[8] The kingdom of God is already partially here, not-yet completely here. It seems that the tension is "some" versus "all"—already some of the kingdom, not-yet all of the kingdom. To a certain degree this is a helpful way of seeing it. But "partial" versus "complete" misses the good news in Jesus' "at hand."

The good news is that the "already, not-yet" is a matter of "veiled" versus "visible." The "already, not-yet" is a matter of "hidden" versus "manifest."[9] The *really* good news is that in Jesus the new order is already among us, but in a veiled, hidden form. It is not-yet among us in a visible, manifest form. That is the mystery of the kingdom which Jesus taught in his parables (see especially Matthew 13).

The presence of the kingdom cannot be separated from the presence of the King. The kingdom is wherever the King is. So right after announcing that the kingdom of God is at hand, Jesus says to four fishermen, "Come, follow me." He and the kingdom are one. When the King is present, so is the kingdom. Indeed, the kingdom is present only where Jesus Christ is King.

Jesus Christ the King has already come. And yet Jesus Christ the King is still to come. We might say Jesus himself is "already, not-yet."

So what is the nature of his "already, not-yet-ness"? Is it a matter of partial versus complete?

No. Jesus Christ is not partially here. He is already completely here. But he is here in *hidden* form. He is *veiled*, or as I should say, ordinarily veiled. Yet hidden and veiled though he may be, he is *really* and *completely* here. The King is here—right where you are—in all his glory, splendor and power: in your home and in your office and in your hospital room. Jesus Christ is at hand, just behind that thin, permeable veil of hiddenness. If God wanted to, he could pull back that veil and we would all be on our knees.

Because the King has come, the kingdom has come. Because the King is still to come, the kingdom is still to come. Because the King is here, the kingdom is here. But since the King is here in veiled form, the kingdom is ordinarily present in veiled form. Is that not why Jesus so often speaks of "having eyes to see and ears to hear"? Not everyone recognizes his already-ness. So not everyone will recognize the already-ness of the reign of God.

This is so important that I want to come at this "already not-yet" from another angle. Take note of the words the New Testament uses for the second coming of Jesus Christ. His return is called the *parousia*, meaning "presence" or "arrival." His return is also called the *epiphaneia*, meaning "appearing," and his return is called the "apocalypse." In our time apocalyse has come to mean, "Oh no, something terrible is about to happen!" But that wasn't the case in the first century. The word simply meant "unveiling." It referred to the pulling back of a curtain, to the lifting of a cover.[10] It means "breaking through from hiddenness." At the end of this age, on the Day of the Lord, God will unveil before the world what is true right now. On that day God will make visible to all people what is true right now: that the crucified carpenter is on the throne of the universe, that the crucified one is now King over all kings and queens, even if those kings and queens do not acknowledge the fact or obey him (Phil 2:9; Eph 1:20-23; Heb 1:3; 2:9; Rev 16). What will break through on that Day is the present Kingly rule of Jesus Christ. At the apocalypse, Jesus' present, but ordinarily veiled, power and glory will be made visible to all (1 Cor 1:7; 2 Thes 1:7; 1 Pet 1:7, 13.). "What the church now awaits is not something more complete than Christ himself, but rather Christ manifest and in glory."[11]

You can see that the term "second coming" is a bit misleading, for he is not coming from some far away place. He is breaking through from behind the veil of hidden-ness. When he does, the already present, but ordinarily hidden, kingdom of God will be manifest to all and will overcome and replace all other kingdoms.

So, what does it mean to pray, "your kingdom come, on earth as it is in heaven"? It means something like "Living God, even before the Day of the Lord, reveal what is invisible, manifest what is hidden."

Can you handle that? That is what those words mean. We ought to pray the words standing on tiptoe!

"Father, your reign of light and joy and power and justice and wholeness is now veiled. O God, unveil your kingdom here on earth just as it is in heaven! King of Kings, break through the veil of hiddenness and manifest your royal splendor and might and healing and goodness."

We mere human beings . . . *we* can ask for the unveiling of the kingdom of God? Yes! If the Church of Jesus has been given this privilege then why haven't we exercised it more intentionally? Perhaps it is because we have not understood the privilege. Perhaps it is that we have not wanted to submit our lives to the King. We may have wanted the benefits and blessings of the kingdom but we have not been willing to align our lives with his rule. Or perhaps it is that we know the coming of God's rule means the end of our rule. Perhaps the church has not fervently prayed for the kingdom because we know it is dangerous to do so; the King just might answer and start turning everything upside-down!

This is what is happening in the world today. The prayer *is* being answered. This is a *kairos* time. The kingdom of God in Jesus Christ is coming, pressing in on the world from every side. Unsettling the status quo. We are in what the apostle Paul called "the birth pangs of redemption" (Rom 8:18-25). The baby has been conceived and is kicking in the womb and is about to be delivered. It is "at hand." We are on the verge of the delivery. And in the mystery of things, praying the Lord's Prayer is part of the process by which it all happens.

What an incredible privilege, to serve the world as midwives, as labor coaches, praying, "your kingdom come." Will you do it today and in the days to come? Will you dare to invite the invasion of heaven on earth?

Will you pray for the kingdom to come *in you*?

"Father, manifest the already-ness of your rule in my life. Break through any darkness; King Jesus, illuminate every corner of my life with your healing light. Father, break through any resistance in my soul; King Jesus, humble me, forgive me, cleanse me. Father, break the bondage that enslaves me; King Jesus, free me, restore

me. Father in heaven, break through the patterns of my life that support or perpetuate injustice; King Jesus, give me courage to follow you come what may."

Will you pray for the kingdom to come through you?

"Father in heaven, manifest the already-ness of your rule through my life; I am yours, I make myself available to you for your purposes in the world. King Jesus, through me, make yourself real in my part of the world; make me an instrument of your peace."

Will you pray for the kingdom to come in and through your church and the other churches of your city or town?

"Father in heaven, make us, your church, a clear and engaging sign that the future is breaking into the present. Grant, O God, that when the city looks at us, it sees you and your new world order. King Jesus, do through us what you did when you walked the earth in visible form. Through us heal the sick, free the captives, reconcile enemies, raise the dead to newness of life."

This—and so much more—is what it means to pray the second petition of the Lord's Prayer. "Bring it on! Bring on your revolution. *Reverse* the effects of sin. *Restore* broken humanity. Come and reign without rival in all the earth!"

4

FULFILL ALL YOUR
GOOD PLEASURES

Our Father in heaven,
your will be done on earth
as it is in heaven.

The older I get the more I want to pray this third petition of the Lord's Prayer. There are two reasons for this. First, the older I get the more I realize I do not know how to make life work. There was a time when I thought I did know. But the world is becoming increasingly complex. I am becoming more aware of the complex interplay between the mind and the heart and the body and the feelings and fears. I look back on a number of turning points in my life, and now rejoice that "my will" was not done. As good as it might have been, "my will" was not as well informed as I thought. I like how Helmut Thielicke put it,

In the last analysis we know very little about our real needs, about what we lack and what we need. So we often pray for foolish things, when what we need is something totally different. We are naked, and instead of praying for clothing we pray for bonbons. We are imprisoned by certain passions . . . and instead of praying for freedom we pray for a Persian rug for our cell. So often we pray for senseless things that have no relation to our needs. And the reason is that we do not know the deepest wants and necessities of our life at all.[1]

"O Father, you do know. Your will be done!"

Second, I am more and more wanting to *pray* the third petition of the Lord's Prayer because I am discovering how *good* the will of God is. The apostle Paul exhorts the disciples in Rome: "Do not conform to the pattern of this world, but be transformed by the renewing of your mind. Then you will be able to test and approve what God's will is—his good, pleasing and perfect will" (Rom 12:2). The more I understand what the Father of Jesus is on about in the world, the more I realize that I am foolish not to want the Father's will done "on earth as it is in heaven."

Are we surprised that Jesus should teach us to pray, "Your will be done" given what we see and hear in Jesus' life and ministry? What are the first recorded words out of Jesus' mouth (at age twelve)? Jesus had gone to Jerusalem with his family for the Passover. After the feast, his family was well on their way home to Nazareth, only to discover that Jesus was not with them. His mother looked everywhere for him, returning to Jerusalem searching all the likely places a 12-year-old boy would hang out. She eventually finds him in the temple, of all places, listening to and questioning the elders. His mother says to him, "Son, why have you treated us like this? Your father and I have been anxiously searching for you." To which Jesus replies, "Why were you searching for me? Didn't you know I had to be about *my Father's business?*" (Luke 2:41-50, KJV).

When Jesus was age thirty or so, he was near the village of Sychar in Samaria. Jesus' disciples are concerned that he has not eaten anything for a while. "Rabbi, eat something," they say. To which Jesus replies, "I have food to eat that you know nothing about." The disciples say to each other, "Could someone have brought him food?" To which Jesus says, "My food is to do the *will of him who sent me* and to finish his work" (John 4:31-34). Yes, Jesus does eat normal food; but that which sustains him is doing the Father's will.

Again, while teaching one day in a crowded building, Jesus is told that his mother and brothers are standing outside wanting to speak to him. They are concerned that he was "going off the deep end." Jesus responds, "Who is my mother, and who are my brothers?" And "pointing to his disciples, he said, 'Here are my mother and my brothers. For whoever does the *will* of my Father in heaven is my brother and sister and mother'" (Matt 12:46-50).

At the age of thirty-three or so, Jesus is under the shadow of the crucifixion, in the Garden of Gethsemane, just outside the city of Jerusalem. Agonizing into the night, sweat like drops of blood falling to the ground, he cries out, "My Father, if it is possible, may this cup be taken from me. Yet not as I will, but as *you will*" (Matt 26:39-42). And a little while later, a second time, "Father, if you are willing, take this cup from me; yet not my will, but yours be done" (Luke 22:40-46).

Thus the writer of the book of Hebrews says of Jesus the Son, "Here I am . . . I have come to do *your will*, my God" (10:7). Jesus lives his whole life in obedience to the Father's will. In other words, Jesus himself embodies what the will of God is all about!

So, of course, he teaches us to pray, "Your will be done." "When you pray, say, Our Father in heaven, your will be done, on earth as it is in heaven."

THE GOODNESS OF GOD'S WILL

Regrettably, many of us pray this third petition of the Lord's Prayer drearily.

"Your name be hallowed"—head up, hands lifted in praise. "Your kingdom come"—eyes open, hands extended in expectation. "Your will be done"—head hanging low, hands to the side.

Some pray the petition with gritted teeth: "Okay, have it your way." Others pray the petition in resignation: "I guess I really do not have any other choice, do I?" Still others pray the petition in resentment: "I do not like this at all, but your will be done."

However, if we understand the will of the Father in the way that Jesus does, we should pray the petition in joyful anticipation.

The word for "will" in "your will be done," conveys the fundamental note of goodness. The word is *thelema*. *Thelema* has the sense of both purpose and *pleasure*.[2] *Thelema* echoes the words of God in Isaiah, "My purpose will be established, I will accomplish all my good pleasure" (46:10, NASB). "Your will be done" means "Your purpose and pleasure be done"; "Your design and delight be done."

This helps to explain the energy and joy that radiates from the opening of the apostle Paul's letter to the Ephesians. Ephesians 1:3-14 is one long sentence celebrating the intense goodness of God. "Praise be to the God and Father of the Lord Jesus Christ, who has blessed us in the heavenly realms with every spiritual blessing in Christ" (1:3). Paul then goes on to identify and elaborate on the most essential of these blessings, and declares that all of this blessing is "according to the *good pleasure* of God's will" (v. 5, NASB). It is referred to again in verse 9, "according to the *good pleasure* of his will," and in verse 11, "according to the plan of him who works out everything in conformity with the purpose of his will" (1:11). Paul is gripped by the goodness of God's will. The Father in heaven, the Father of Jesus, the Father Jesus knows and loves and trusts, has a will for his children, a good and perfect will for you and me, and for the world. "Father in heaven, fulfill all your good pleasures, accomplish your good purposes, on earth as it is in heaven."

Remember what we observed when we began our journey through the Lord's Prayer: we are asking God to do what only God can do. The prayer is not, "let *us* do your will on earth as it is in heaven." This is not a bad thing to pray—not at all! But it is not what Jesus is teaching us in this prayer. The prayer is not even, "Give *us* power, O God, so *we* can do your will." The prayer is not even, "Do a miracle in *our* fearful and rebellious hearts so that *we* will want to do your will." The prayer is, "Father, *you* do your will." The verb is in the imperative, "do it." The verb is in the passive imperative implying *only you* can do it. Only you can hallow your name. Only you can bring in your kingdom. Only you can do your will. "O Father, we are asking you to do what we cannot do, what only you can do. Your purposes and pleasures are being fulfilled in heaven, fulfill them on earth. You are doing your good and perfect will in heaven, do it on *earth*!"

The question is, what is the Father's will, the Father's good pleasures? Is that not what the Bible is all about? Is not the Bible telling the story of God revealing and accomplishing his will? Is not page after page declaring, "These are God's good pleasures"? In the section of the apostle Paul's letter to the Ephesians, which

I referred to earlier, Paul makes the amazing claim that God "has made known to us the mystery of his will" (1:9). God does not hide his will from us. He has gladly revealed it for the entire world to know.

The Father's will is that we humans be as creative as he is. God's first word to humanity is "be fruitful and multiply, and fill the earth, and subdue it" (Gen 1:28). The Father's will is that we humans join him in his governing of the creation. "Rule over the fish in the sea and the birds in the sky, and over every living creature that moves on the ground" (Gen 1:28). Yes, God's words to humanity have been abused, tragically so in some places. But do not let that get in the way of recognizing God's good pleasure: the awesome Creator of the universe delights to have us be as creative as he is. He wills us to write poetry, paint pictures, compose music, build buildings, tend forests, design airplanes and automobiles, assemble intricate electronic wonders. This is God's will for the creatures made in his image.

The Father's will is that we humans be blessed and then bless. After humanity messed up God's good world, God did not give up. Rather God began a plan to repair the world, and redeem his creatures into his good purposes. In Genesis 12:1-3 God called a couple, Abraham and Sarah, from the land of Ur of the Chaldeans, from what is now called Iraq, and God began a work that would ultimately bless the whole world. "I will make you into a great nation, and I will bless you; I will make your name great, and you will be a blessing . . . and all peoples on earth will be blessed through you." The Father's will, the will of the God of Abraham, is to pour out blessing on his people, so that his people can pour out blessings on others. The Father of the Lord Jesus Christ is forming "a culture of blessing."

The Father's will is to set us free from all that keeps us from being blessed so that we can be a blessing. God's will is to free us captives from any and all forms of bondage. Is that not what is being revealed in the central story of the Old Testament, in the Exodus? Exodus 3 is a critical turning point in unfolding God's will. "I have indeed seen the misery of my people . . . I have heard them crying out . . . I am concerned about their sufferings . . . I have come down to rescue them." "Pharaoh, let my people go!" The Father of Jesus finds no pleasure in people being in bondage. His will is that we be free, that we live in the very freedom he enjoys. The Father's good pleasure is that creation be liberated from the powers of sin and evil. The Father finds no pleasure in our chains. Is this not what we see in Jesus' ministry, in the life of him whose food is doing the Father's will? "The Spirit of the Lord is on me, because he has anointed me to proclaim good news to the poor. He has sent me to proclaim freedom for the prisoners and recovery of sight for the blind" (Luke 4:18). We can cry out for freedom from our addictions because this is the very thing the Father desires and wills.

The Father's will is that we grow into this freedom, which is why he spoke the Ten Commandments. The Law is given not to tie us up but to release us into the fullness of freedom. How do the commandments do this? By telling us who we are, by revealing who we were created to be. As E. Stanley Jones, the Methodist missionary to India, put it: the commandments are not an imposition, they are an *exposition*.[3] The commandments are not imposed on the human species from outside us; they expose what is true inside us. "You shall have no other gods before me." Why? Because God is an egoist and cannot handle rivals? No. "You shall have no other gods" because we were created in such a way that only the one, true, Living God can satisfy us. We finite creatures were made in such a way that only the Infinite God can fill and fulfill us. God speaks the commandment to protect us, to keep us from ruining our lives by seeking satisfaction in what ultimately does not satisfy. "Remember the Sabbath day by keeping it holy. Six days you shall labour and do all your work, but the seventh day is a sabbath to the LORD your God." Why this commandment? Because God is against work? Because work is not spiritual enough? No. The commandment is not an imposition but an *exposition*. The commandment reveals something about the human creature we would never deduce: we are built in such a way that we live fully human by working six days a week and resting one. God speaks the commandment to protect and enhance our free enjoyment of our creatureliness.

The Father's will is that we live the kingdom life. The Father's will is, therefore, that we live Jesus' Sermon on the Mount, where he describes humanity "alive" in his kingdom. Again, the commandments of the Sermon on the Mount are not impositions but *expositions*. Matthew tells us that after Jesus preached his Sermon, a sermon that cut against the grain of everything we know, the people were amazed "because he taught as one who had authority, and not as their teachers of the law" (7:29). This word translated "authority" is the word *exousia*. It is made up of two words: *ek* (ex) meaning "out of," and *ousi* meaning "being." *Exousia* thus means "out of being," "the really real."[4]

"Love your enemies and pray for those who persecute you" (Matt 5:44). Why? Because hating our enemies goes against reality. Eye for eye, tooth for tooth, insult for insult, missile for missile, goes against reality. Only love is *exousia*, out of being. Jesus calls us to this radical and different way of life because he wants us to be alive, alive in the kingdom. The Father does not want us to get sucked in the downward spiral of retaliation and hate.

Do you see why the apostle Paul says the will of God is good and perfect?

The Father's will is that we know him. This is the essence of the New Covenant sealed in Jesus' blood. Jeremiah 31:33-34 says, "This is the covenant I will make . . . I will put my law in their minds and write it on their hearts. I will be their God, and they will be my people. No longer will they teach their neighbors, or say to one another, 'know the LORD,' because they will all *know me* . . . for I will forgive their wickedness and will remember their sins no more." The word for *know* (*yadah*) used in, "They shall all know me," is the same word used for a husband and wife knowing each other in marital intimacy. That is the will of God—that we know him in such intimacy! That we know the Father as Jesus knows him. That we know Jesus as the Father knows him. That we love the Father the way Jesus loves him. That we love Jesus the way the Father loves him.[5]

The Father's will is that we be filled with his life. The will of God, the good pleasure of God, is that his very life be in us. "Do not be foolish," says Paul in his letter to the Ephesians, "but understand what the Lord's will is." And it is this: "Be filled with the Spirit" (Eph 5:17-18). The Holy Spirit is the embodiment of the relationship between the Father and Jesus. The Holy Spirit is the embodiment of the love that flows between the Father and Jesus. And it is the will of God that we be filled with that Spirit! It is the will of God that the Triune God himself take up residence in us!

Which is how the Father's will that we be holy is fulfilled. "You shall be holy, for I the LORD your God am holy." It is the Father's will that we be holy by being filled with a Holy Presence. Only God can make us holy. And he does it by taking up residence in our unholiness, changing us from the inside out.

What is the will of God? What are God's good pleasures? Look at John 6:38-40, the verses that summarize the whole book of John. Jesus is speaking. "For I have come down from heaven not to do my will but to do the will of him who sent me. And this is the will of him who sent me, that I shall lose none of all those he has given me, but raise them up at the last day. For my Father's will is that everyone who looks to the Son and believes in him shall have eternal life, and I will raise them up at the last day."

God's will for us is to look on Jesus Christ. And then believing in him, to receive eternal life. Eternal life is not just long life, life that does not end. Eternal life is the life God has. Eternal life is the life God *is*. And the will of God—"Your will be done on earth as it is in heaven"—is that we receive and experience that eternal life here and now. In so doing we become finally what we were created to be: creatures alive in the Creator; creatures filled with the uncreated life of the Creator.

"He has made known the mystery of his will," says the apostle Paul. It is all over the place, on every page of world history.

And it is finally, as Paul puts it, "the summing up of all things in Christ" (Eph 1:10, NASB). The word translated "summing up" is interesting. It is literally means "recapitulate." Recapitulate means, "to put the head back on." Sin and evil have *de*capitated the human race. As a race we are running around with our heads off. It is the will of God, God's good pleasure, to *recapitulate* the race—to put the Head back on. To reconnect the human species to its proper Head. His will is to recapitulate me, to recapitulate you, and to recapitulate the whole universe!

So who in their right mind would not want to pray, "Your will be done on earth as it is in heaven"? Ah, there is the problem: "right mind." We are not, ordinarily, in our right mind. C.S. Lewis, the brilliant British writer, said it so well in his sermon, *The Weight of*

Glory, preached in 1941. In it he wrestles with the fact that we are suspicious of our desires. And he says this:

> It would seem that Our Lord finds our desires not too strong, but too weak. We are half-hearted creatures, fooling about with drink and sex and ambition when infinite joy is offered us, [we are] like an ignorant child who wants to go on making mud pies in a slum because he cannot imagine what is meant by the offer of a holiday at the sea. We are far too easily pleased.[7]

Who in their right mind would not want the will of the Father of the Lord Jesus done on earth as it is in heaven?

Now we know just how corrupt evil is. It seeks to undo such a wonderful will. Now we know just how sinful our sin is, that it would cause us to turn from and resist such a grand purpose.

And now we know *why Jesus goes to the cross*. He dies to overcome the power of that evil, to break the grip of that sin. Only this explains the agony in the Garden, "Father, if it is possible, may this cup be taken from me." This cup is the cross, where Jesus faces the full power of evil, where Jesus takes on the sin of the world. "If it is possible, may this cup pass from me. Yet not as I will, but as you will. Your will be done."

And it was.

So that the good and well-pleasing and perfect will of the Father can now be realized in us.

And thus it is with joyful anticipation, heads up, hands raised, that we pray, *"Our Father in heaven, your will, your good purpose and perfect pleasures, be done on earth as it is in heaven."*

There are times when praying this third petition my heart wants to sing with Charles Wesley (1747) the words of his hymn "Love Divine." It best captures what the Prayer is all about:

> Love divine, all loves excelling,
> Joy of heaven, to earth come down,

Fix in us Thy humble dwelling,
All Thy faithful mercies crown!
Jesus, Thou art all compassion,
Pure, unbounded love Thou art;
Visit us with Thy salvation,
Enter every trembling heart.

Breathe, O breathe Thy loving Spirit
Into every troubled breast!
Let us all in Thee inherit,
Let us find that second rest;
Take away our bent to sinning;
Alpha and Omega be;
End of faith as its beginning,
Set our hearts at liberty.

Come, Almighty to deliver,
Let us all Thy life receive;
Suddenly return, and nevermore Thy temples leave.
Thee we would be always blessing,
Serve Thee as Thy hosts above;
Pray, and praise Thee without ceasing,
Glory in Thy perfect love.

Finish, then, Thy new creation;
Pure and spotless let us be;
Let us see Thy great salvation
Perfectly restored in Thee;
Changed from glory into glory,
Till in heaven we take our place,
Till we cast our crowns before Thee,
Lost in wonder, love, and praise.

BE OUR PROVIDER

Our Father in heaven, give us this day our daily bread.

B read. We simply cannot make it without bread. Bread (or rice) is the fundamental staple of human existence. We can make it without coffee or chocolate—honestly, we can! We can make it without television or a new wardrobe. But we cannot make it without bread. Jesus says to the devil in the wilderness, "People do not live by bread *alone,* but on every word that comes from the mouth of God" (Matt 4:4). He does not say we can live *without* bread. Without bread we eventually die. So Jesus teaches us to pray, "Our Father in heaven, give us this day our daily bread."

In this fourth petition of the Lord's Prayer, Jesus shifts pronouns. Jesus shifts from "your," to "us" and "our." From *your* name, *your* kingdom, *your* will, to give *us our,* forgive *us our,* lead *us* not, deliver *us.*

It appears that in the shift in pronouns Jesus is changing direction, jumping to another stream, so to speak. It appears that when we move from "your, your, your," to "us, us, us, our, our, our," we are moving, as many commentators put it, from the Father's cause to our cause. In the fourth petition in particular, in "give us this day our daily bread," it appears we have dropped from what is lofty and cosmic to what is mundane and parochial.

But this is not the case at all. As we have made our way through the first three petitions of the Lord's Prayer (i.e., your name be hallowed, your kingdom come, your will be done), we have seen how "earth-bound" each of the "lofty" requests is. We have seen that the central phrase of the Lord's Prayer, "on earth as it is in heaven," belongs with each of the first three petitions. "Your name be hallowed *on earth*, your kingdom come *on earth*, your will be done *on earth*." The first three petitions are about earthly, and *earthy*, realities. To then pray about bread is, therefore, not to veer off course; we are not leaving something behind.

We human beings are material creatures and cannot enter into and enjoy the fulfillment of the first three petitions without bread. The Father's will is that his name be made manifest to flesh and blood men and women, not just to angels. The Father's will is that his kingdom be made real among finite, physical creatures, not just among disembodied spirits. We do not enter into and enjoy the Father's name being hallowed, the Father's kingdom coming, the Father's will being done, as souls. We enter into and enjoy these things as souls *in* bodies, as embodied souls with bodies that need daily bread.

In shifting pronouns Jesus has not jumped streams at all; he has not shifted "causes" or subjects.[1] The subject of "bread," in particular, is a natural extension of the subject of "the kingdom of God." The dominant biblical symbol of the kingdom is "the great festive banquet."[2] Thus in the story of the Exodus, to which we have referred throughout our journey in the Lord's Prayer, God calls his people out of bondage and poverty in Egypt to a land "flowing with milk and honey." And along the way God feeds his people quail by night and manna by day. Manna "from heaven," sweet tasting bread from heaven. And he does so everyday for forty years! In abundance!

Not surprisingly, then, when the Old Testament prophets longed for the great Day of the Lord they thought in terms of a banquet. Isaiah 25:6 says, "The LORD Almighty will prepare a feast of rich foods for all peoples, a banquet of aged wine—the best of meats and the finest of wines." King David sings in Psalm 23, "The LORD is my shepherd, I lack nothing. . . . You prepare a table before me in the presence of my enemies."

What stood out about Jesus' ministry to people of the first century? Miracles, yes. But mostly that he was always celebrating with people, at meals around tables spread with fruits and breads. At one of those many meals Jesus said, "I am among you as one who serves" (Luke 22:27). Jesus sees himself as a waiter at tables.[3] He "sees to it" that people are fed. The one miracle all four Gospel writers record is the feeding of the 5,000 when Jesus took five loaves and two fish and multiplied them, serving hungry people with an abundance of bread. How many of his parables are about eating bread? How many times did he compare the kingdom of God to a banquet? "Many will come from the east and the west, and will take their places at the feast with Abraham, Isaac and Jacob in the kingdom of heaven" (Matt 8:11).

How natural then, for Jesus, the bringer of the kingdom, to teach us to pray "give us this day our daily bread," right on the heels of teaching us to pray "your kingdom come on earth." We have not dropped from the lofty to the mundane at all.

This fourth petition raises a host of good questions. Questions like:[4] is it right for us who have more than "daily bread" to pray this prayer? Does such praying have integrity? Do we really need to pray this prayer given God's commitment to creation and humanity? Isn't praying this prayer a lot like asking God to keep the earth turning and revolving around the sun? Questions like: what about the millions of hungry, starving people in the world today; do not some of them pray this prayer? Then why do they go without bread? Is it that too many of us who prayed this prayer are hoarding the answer to the prayer? How can "daily bread" be considered a gift of the Father of Jesus "when it comes from the market as a result of the hard work of farmers and bakers?" And questions like: how is praying for "daily bread" related to what Jesus teaches us in the section of his Sermon on the Mount which follows the Lord's Prayer? How does praying the prayer relate to the exhortation, "Do not worry about your life, what you will eat or drink . . . So do not worry, saying, 'What shall we eat?'" (Matt 6:25, 31).

We get at answers to such questions by focusing them all into two questions. *Question one*: what is it that Jesus is teaching us to ask for in the fourth petition? *Question two*: what are the life-style implications of praying this petition? Essentially, what does the prayer mean and, if we authentically pray it, what will happen to the way we live?

Before we answer these questions we need to deal with the word translated "daily." Different versions of the Bible render the term differently. Some render it, "give us this day our daily bread." Some, however, render it, "give us this day our bread for the coming day." Why the difference? Because of the Greek word used in Matthew 6:11. It is the word *epiousion*. The problem is that this is the only place in the Bible where the word is used. As far as we know, it is the only place in the whole of Greek literature where it is used! *Epiousion* is a compound word, made up of a preposition—*epi*, meaning "for, towards, upon"—and a connected participle. The question is, a participle of what verb? Is it the participle of the verb "to be," *ousion?* Or is it the participle of the verb "to come," *iousion?* (As William Barclay puts it, "There is only an iota of difference."[5]) Is the word a compound of *epi* plus the participle of *be* and *being, ousion?* Or is the word a compound of *epi* plus the participle of *come* and *coming, iousion?* Is it bread for the *being* day? Or is it bread for the *coming* day?

The most likely answer is *coming*, "bread for the coming day." Why? When *epi* is combined with *ousion* (being), the "i" (iota) drops, making for *epousion*. When *epi* is combined with *iousion* (coming), one of the "i"s (iota) drops, making for *epiousion*. "Give us this day the bread for the coming day." If it is prayed in the morning we are asking for bread for today. If it is prayed in the evening, we are asking for bread for tomorrow.[6] Either way, we are praying for our immediate needs. The focus is the next twenty-four hours of life.

QUESTION ONE

Question one: what does the prayer mean? Over the centuries the church has come to realize that the prayer has a *wide* range of meanings. It turns out that this "simple prayer" casts as wide a net as do the first three petitions!

Consider what some of those who have prayed the Lord's Prayer before us in church history have said about the meaning of the fourth petition.

Martin Luther, early in the sixteenth century, in one of his catechisms (a discipleship tool) asks, "What is meant by daily bread?" He answers, "'Daily bread' means everything we need for our bodily well-being." He goes on to suggest that it includes "food, drink, clothes, shoes, house, home, land, animals, money and goods, a godly husband or wife, devout children, good workers, honest and faithful leaders, good government, good weather, peace, health, law and order, an honorable name, faithful friends, trustworthy neighbors and things like that."[7]

Another perspective comes from the Westminster Larger Catechism, compiled in 1674 by the Westminster Assembly, which sought to renew the Church of England. Question 193 is, "What do we pray for in the fourth petition?" Answer:

> In the fourth petition (which is, "give us this day our daily bread") acknowledging, that in Adam, and by our own sin, we have forfeited our right to all the outward blessings of this life, and deserve to be wholly deprived of them by God, and to have them cursed to us in the use of them; and that neither they of themselves are able to sustain us, nor we to merit, or by our own industry to procure them; but prone to desire, get, and use them unlawfully: we pray for ourselves and others, that both they and we, waiting upon the providence of God from day to day in the use of lawful means, may, of his free gift, and as to his fatherly wisdom shall seem best, enjoy a competent portion of them; and have the same continued and blessed unto us in our holy and comfortable use of them, and contentment in them; and be kept from all things that are contrary to our temporal support and comfort.

Another example can be found in the Westminster Shorter Catechism. Question 104 is, "What do we pray for in the fourth petition?" Answer: "In the fourth petition, which is, 'Give us this day our daily bread,' we pray that, of God's free gift, we may receive a competent portion of the good things of this life, and enjoy his blessing with them."

Yet one more perspective may be found in the Heidelberg Catechism of 1563, greatly influencing the Netherlands of the sixteenth through nineteenth centuries. It asks, "What is the fourth petition?" Answer:

> "Give us this day our daily bread." That is: be pleased to provide us with all our bodily needs so that we may acknowledge that thou art the only source of all that is good, and that without thy blessing neither our care and labor nor thy gifts can do us any good. Therefore, may we withdraw our trust from all creatures and place it in thee alone.

As we read the church's reflection on this petition, we find six layers of meaning, each one having biblical support.

The first layer is *physical bread*: food in general, fuel so the body can work.

The second layer is *everything necessary* for functioning in the world. Again, Martin Luther: "Everything necessary for the preservation of this life." It is a prayer for a balanced diet—for more than bread—for vegetables and meat and milk. And for all that comprises a balanced diet. It is a prayer for weather patterns enabling crops to grow in abundance. It is a prayer for wisdom and strength for farmers who plant and nurture and harvest the crops. It is a prayer for truckers who move the crops from the farms to the producing plants and then to the markets. It is a prayer for CEOs of companies that oversee the movement of goods. It is a prayer for grocery clerks and those who stock the shelves. It is a prayer for those who cook the food and serve the meals. My friend Dale Bruner calls the fourth petition of the Lord's Prayer the "political-economic prayer."[8] We are asking the Father to attend to and sustain the whole process, from the planting of seeds in the ground to the placing of baked bread on the table. "Daily bread": everything necessary for the preservation of life.

The third layer is everything necessary *for living the kingdom life*. Bread, yes. But also wisdom, courage, strength, patience, holiness, and vision—especially vision. "Father, we want to seek first your kingdom; we want to be kingdom people in the world. Keep our vision clear. Do not let it dim. Give us courage to follow the kingdom way, the way of the cross."

"Give us *today* our daily bread." "Today" because *today* is the day we are to live the kingdom life. After his sermon in the synagogue of Nazareth, Jesus said, "*Today* this Scripture is fulfilled in your hearing" (Luke 4:21). After having a meal with Zacchaeus the tax collector during which Zacchaeus repents of his corrupt, unjust ways, Jesus says, "*Today* salvation has come to this house" (Luke 19:9). The apostle Paul, after declaring the glory of the Gospel, that God has reconciled the world to himself in Jesus, says, "*Now* is the day of salvation" (2 Cor 6:2). "Father, give us today the bread, the resources, we need to live in the 'today' of the kingdom."

The fourth layer is spiritual bread, the *resources of the Holy Spirit*, enabling us to live in faith, hope, and love. So Jesus says, "People do not live on bread alone, but on every word that comes from the mouth of God." We need bread from his hand, and sustenance from his mouth. "The words I have spoken to you," says Jesus, "they are full of the Spirit and life" (John 6:63). And so we have ministries such as *Daily Bread* and other daily devotionals that help us feed on the words of life. An old hymn puts it this way:

> Break Thou the bread of life, dear Lord to me,
> As Thou didst break the loaves beside the sea;
> Beyond the sacred page I seek Thee, Lord,
> My spirit pants for Thee, O living Word.[9]

So, the fifth layer of meaning is *Jesus himself*. It means "Father, give us this day Jesus, the Bread of Life." "I am the bread of life.

Whoever comes to me will never go hungry, and whoever believes in me will never be thirsty" (John 6:35). It is one of the boldest, most audacious claims he ever made. "New York—London—Shanghai, you need me more that you need your next meal." Jesus also said, "Do not work for the food that spoils, but for food that endures to eternal life, which the Son of Man will give you" (John 6:27). And it turns out to be himself. Psalm 63 says, "I thirst for you, my whole being longs for you." He is what I need more than anything else. Nothing else satisfies the ravenous hunger.

Is it a mere coincidence that he is born in Bethlehem? *Beth* means house; *lehem* means bread. Bethlehem means "house of bread," where the Father gives the bread of life to the world. John 6 again, verses 46-50, "I am the bread of life. Your ancestors ate the manna in the wilderness, yet they died. But here is the bread that comes down from heaven, which people may eat and not die."

The sixth layer of meaning is *bread for "the coming day,"* for the so-called "eschatological day," the final day when the kingdom of God comes in all its fullness. "Father, give us today the bread we will enjoy in your fully realized kingdom. Give us today the delicious bread of peace, joy, rest." And are there not moments when we actually taste this bread? Moments when something of that future day breaks into the present and we are given strength and courage to keep going?

So, what is it that Jesus teaches us to pray for in the fourth petition? For physical bread. For everything necessary for functioning in this world. For everything we need to live a kingdom life. For spiritual sustenance. For Jesus himself! For something of the glorious future when we shall never hunger again.

Now remember why Jesus teaches us the Lord's Prayer: to free us from the burden of wondering if our prayers are acceptable to God. Jesus is saying, "Here is prayer that pleases my Father. Ask for all that is meant by 'bread.'"

QUESTION TWO

Question two: if we authentically pray this prayer, what happens to the way we live? I can see three major life-style implications.

First, praying the fourth petition, "Give us this day our daily bread," calls us to a life-style of *solidarity*. Note the pronouns carefully. "Give *us, our* daily bread"—they are plural. Not "give *me, my* daily bread." Not even "give my family." Not even "give my church." But give us—the "us" being all those who have become children of the Father through faith in Jesus. "Us" refers to all the brothers and sisters of Jesus in the world. To pray the fourth petition of the Lord's Prayer is to enter into solidarity with the whole family of God. "Give us, Father." My family, but also my neighbor's family, and the Lopez family of Guatemala, and the Kim family of Korea, and the Lee family of Singapore, and the Punanbayan family of Philippines, and the MacDonald family of Scotland. "Give *us*" is the logical extension of "*our* Father." The "us" keeps the prayer from self-centered-ness. The "us" keeps us socially aware. The "us" makes us kingdom-conscious.

Can you imagine how different the world would be if we prayed the "us" with greater integrity? One of the scandals of our time is the huge disparity in basic life-provisions in the Body of Christ. Many disciples of Jesus have more than we can possibly use, and worry about how to protect it. Many more disciples of Jesus wonder how to take care of the minimal needs of their families and yet, ironically, seek to share what little they have. A Latin American prayer puts it this way: "O God, to those who have hunger give bread; and to those who have bread (give) the hunger for justice."[10] To pray "give *us*" leads us into solidarity with the whole family of God.

Second, praying the fourth petition—"give us this day our daily bread"—calls us to a life-style of radical *dependency* on the Father of the Lord Jesus. "Daily" bread, says Jesus. Not "weekly," not "monthly." But "daily." The prayer calls us to live "one day at a time." In the first century this was the only way people lived. There were no refrigerators. Some were able to store crops in barns. But even they felt vulnerable against the elements. In our century we do not feel this "one day at a time" as keenly. And, therefore, we can more easily fall into the illusion that we are the providers. Until the storms come. Until drought hits. And then we do not know how to cope. "Daily" bread, "day by day, one day at a time." Always dependent upon the goodness and faithfulness of God.

Jesus likely has the Exodus story in mind again. When the people of God traveled across the desert from Egypt to the Promised Land, God provided manna, one day at a time, for forty years. The heads of families were to gather a certain amount for each person living in his tent. The text says, "The Israelites did as they were told; some gathered much, some little" (Exod 16:17). And then the text says, "When they measured it . . . the one who gathered much did not have too much, and the one who had gathered little did not have too little" (16:18). The people were to eat their portion of the manna the day they gathered it; they were not to horde it. The text says, "Some of them paid no attention to Moses; they kept part of it until morning, but it was full of maggots and began to smell" (16:20). *Daily bread.* Enough for each new day. Every day in abundance.

75

But just for that one day. The people of God were having to depend on God one day at a time.

As I pray the fourth petition, my mind keeps going to the prayer of Proverbs 30:7-9, the prayer my wife Sharon and I prayed when we were married in 1971. "Two things I asked of you, do not refuse me before I die: Keep deception and lies far from me, give me neither poverty nor riches. Feed me the food that is my portion, lest I be full and deny Thee and say, 'Who is the Lord?'; or lest I be in want and steal, and profane the name of my God" (NASB). Enough so we are not tempted to take life into our own hands and steal; but not so much that we are tempted to think life is in our own hands and feel no need to pray.

Praying this "one day at a time" prayer, of course, poses a crisis of faith. Is the Father of Jesus *able* to provide one day at a time? Is the Father of Jesus *faithful* to provide? Will he come through tomorrow and the next day, and the next day, until we are finally in the Promised Land?

What do we see in the life and ministry of Jesus? *He* is the embodiment of the Father's will. What do we see in *him*? How many times did the fishermen fish all night and catch nothing? Then Jesus comes along the seashore and yells out, "Cast your nets on the other side of the boat"—and the fishermen were not able to haul in the nets because they were so full (See Luke 5:5-7; John 21:3-6, 11). Jesus is able to pull out of the sea what others cannot! How many times did the multitudes gather to hear him teach and find themselves hungry for food? And how many times did he take whatever was available and from it make more? Jesus is able to take whatever we have and multiply it! Each time there were baskets full of leftovers. The wine runs out at a wedding feast in Cana of Galilee, and Jesus turns water into wine. It is the greatest miracle of provision, for the ingredients for the wine were not in the water. It is one thing to pull fish out of the sea for the fish were already there; he just knows how to find them. It is another thing to multiply loaves of bread, for he makes more of what is already there. But it is another thing altogether to make wine out of water, for the ingredients for the wine are not there. *Jesus is able to bring into being something out of nothing.*

Yes, God is able. More than able. As Annie Johnson Flint sings, "When we reach the end of our hoarded resources, our Father's full giving is only begun."[11] *We* think we will have peace of mind if we ask God to provide *today* what we need for the future. But, as Dallas Willard points out, to have provisions in hand today does not guarantee we will have them tomorrow when we need them. Willard writes, "Today I have God, and he has the provisions. Tomorrow it will be the same. I will have God and he will have the provisions. So I simply ask God today for what I need for today."[12]

Solidarity with the whole family of God. *Dependency* on God, one day at a time.

And third, to pray the fourth petition, "give us this day our daily bread," calls us to a lifestyle of *gratitude*. Every time we take bread in our hands we are handling an answered prayer. Do you realize that? Do I? Every piece of bread, or bowl of rice, or slice of cheese, or bite of apple, is an answer to someone's prayer. Every time the crops come up, is an answer to someone's prayer. Every time the food makes it from the farm to the store shelf, it is an answer to someone's prayer. The only appropriate response is "thank you." *"Thank you, Father, for once again providing. Thank you, Father, for once again making your good earth work. Thank you for once again being faithful to your children."*

Every time we see or hear the name "Jesus" we are seeing and hearing answered prayer, for he is finally that without which we cannot live. The only appropriate response is "thank you." *"Thank you, Father, for so loving the world that you gave us your only begotten Son, the bread of life, that we should not perish but have everlasting life."*

6

CANCEL ALL OUR DEBTS

Our Father in heaven, forgive us our debts,
as we also have forgiven our debtors.

Forgive us our debts. In my opinion, this is the *boldest* petition of the Lord's Prayer. Indeed, in my opinion, it is the boldest prayer anyone can ever pray. It is rivaled only by the apostle Paul's prayer in Ephesians 3:19, asking that we be "filled to the measure of all the fullness of God." O Father, Creator and Judge of the universe, forgive us our debts . . ."

"As we also have forgiven our debtors." In my opinion, it is also the most *arresting* clause in the Lord's Prayer—indeed, one of the most arresting and disturbing things Jesus ever said. It is the only part of the Prayer that Jesus singles out for further comment. "For if you forgive others when they sin against you, your heavenly Father will also forgive you. But if you do not forgive others their sins, your Father will not forgive your sins" (6:14-15).

"Our Father in heaven, forgive us our debts, as we also have forgiven our debtors."

As you likely know, different Christian traditions word this fifth petition of the Lord's Prayer differently. Some pray, "Forgive us our debts, as we forgive our debtors." Some, in light of Jesus' use of the word "transgression" in his elaboration, pray, "Forgive us our transgressions, as we forgive those who transgress against us." Some, following the version of the prayer in Luke 11, pray, "Forgive us our sins, for we ourselves also forgive everyone who sins against us." And some, following the New English Bible, pray, "Forgive us the wrong we have done, as we have forgiven those who have wronged us."

The word translated "debt" in Matthew 6:12 (*opheilemata*, the plural of *opheilema*),[1] "is a word with a wide range of meanings, all grouped around one common and unchanging idea."[2] New Testament scholar William Barclay writes, "It always denotes something which is owed, something which is due, something which is a duty or an obligation to give or to pay. In other words, it means a debt in the widest sense of the term."[3]

The word used here in Matthew's version of the prayer comes not from the religious realm of life, but from the commercial realm. In its narrowest sense the word refers to a financial debt. More widely, it refers to any social or moral obligation that is a person's duty to discharge.[4]

Interestingly, the word "forgive" also does not come from the religious realm, but from the world of commerce. At its root it means to cancel, to wipe the slate clean, to erase numbers in a business ledger. "Father in heaven, forgive us our debts; erase from the ledger every failure of duty to you and to our fellow humans; cancel the debts we owe to you and to our fellow humans."

Jesus uses this very language and imagery in his parable on forgiveness in Matthew 18. Jesus teaches it in response to Peter's question, "Lord, how many times shall I forgive someone who sins against me? Up to seven times?" (18:21). Peter is, in his mind, being hugely magnanimous. Seven times! Jesus responds, "I tell you, not seven times, but seventy-seven times" (18:22). Have you ever wondered why these numbers are seven and seventy-seven? Because of what a man named Lamech once said. Lamech, great, great, great . . . grandson of Cain, the first born child of Adam and Eve, had been wounded in some way by a young boy. In Genesis 4 Lamech sings a song that ends, "If Cain is avenged seven times, then Lamech seventy-seven times" (4:24). The numbers "seven" and "seventy-seven" on the lips of Peter and Jesus speak of the reversal of the natural human tendency toward resentment and revenge, a reversal which Jesus has come to effect in the human soul. Then Jesus teaches his parable (Matt 18:23-35, NASB):

> For this reason, the kingdom of heaven may be compared to a certain king who wished to settle accounts with his slaves. And when he had begun to settle them, there was brought to him one who owed him ten thousand talents [about 10 million dollars]. But since he did not have the means to repay, his lord commanded him to be sold, along with his wife and children and all that he had, and repayment to be made. The slave therefore falling down, prostrated himself before him saying "have patience with me and I will repay you everything" [How will he repay 10 million dollars?!]. And the lord of that slave felt compassion and released him and forgave him the debt. But that slave went out and found one of his fellow-slaves who owed him a hundred denarii [about one hundred dollars]; and he seized him and began to choke him, saying, "Pay back what you owe." So his fellow-slave fell down and began to entreat him, saying, "Have patience with me and I will repay you." He was unwilling however, but went and threw him in prison until

he should pay back what was owed. So when his fellow-slaves saw what had happened, they were deeply grieved and came and reported to their lord all that had happened. Then summoning him, his lord said to him, "You wicked slave, I forgave you all that debt because you entreated me. Should you not also have had mercy on your fellow-slave, even as I had mercy on you?" And his lord, moved with anger, handed him over to the torturers until he should repay all that was owed him. So shall my heavenly Father also do to you, if each of you does not forgive his brother [or sister] from your heart.

"Father in heaven, cancel our debts, as we also have canceled the debts of others."

What is the debt we owe? In a word, it is obedience: the "obedience of faith," as the apostle Paul puts it in his letter to the Romans (1:5, 16:26, NASB). We owe God trust that ensues in obedience. Not to trust God by not obeying God is to "be in debt" to God. We are in debt for all our failures to obey. It is an overwhelming and horrendous debt. As Helmut Thielicke put it: "All of us have a great mortgage upon our life."[5]

Just for a moment feel the weight of our indebtedness. I say, "Just for a moment," because to feel the weight longer would crush us. In order to begin to feel the size of the mortgage on our lives, we should read the Ten Commandments. "You shall have no other gods before me." You shall not let anything or anyone come between you and me. "You shall not make for yourselves an idol." You shall not try to imagine me in your own terms. "Remember the Sabbath day by keeping it holy." "Honor your father and your mother." "You shall not murder." "You shall not commit adultery." "You shall not steal." "You shall not give false testimony." "You shall not covet." We are all undone here. "You shall not covet your neighbor's house; you shall not covet your neighbor's wife or his male or female servant, his ox or donkey, or anything that belongs to your neighbor."

Read Job 31. Job protests the way he is being treated, claiming he is innocent. I read what Job claims and I hang my head in shame. "I made a covenant with my eyes not to look lustfully at a virgin" (31:1). "If I have walked with falsehood or my foot has hurried after deceit . . ." (31:5). "If I have denied the desires of the poor or let the eyes of the widow grow weary, if I have kept my bread to myself, not sharing it with the fatherless . . ." (31:16-17). "If I have seen anyone perishing for lack of clothing, or the needy without garments, and their hearts did not bless me for warming them with the fleece from my sheep . . ." (31:19). "If I have put my confidence in gold, and called gold my fine thirst" (31:24).

Read what Jesus calls us to in the sections of his Sermon on the Mount, before he teaches the Lord's Prayer:

> "You have heard that it was said to the people long ago, 'You shall not murder, and anyone who murders will be subject to judgment.' But I tell you that anyone who is angry with a brother or sister will be subject to judgment. Again, anyone who says to a brother or sister, 'Raca,' [empty-headed, good for nothing] is answerable to the Sanhedrin. And anyone who says, 'You fool!' will be in danger of the fire of hell. (Matt 5:21-22)

> "You have heard that it was said, 'You shall not commit adultery.' But I tell you that anyone who looks at a woman lustfully has already committed adultery with her in his heart. (Matt 5:27-28)

> "You have heard that it was said, 'Love your neighbor and hate your enemy.' But I tell you, love your enemies and pray for those who persecute you, that you may be children of your Father in heaven. He causes his sun to rise on the evil and the good, and sends rain on the righteous and the unrighteous. (Matt 5:43-45)

Every failure to live up to these kingdom obligations puts us "in debt." What a mammoth debt I owe! A titanic mortgage!

Origen (an early church father who lived from about A.D. 185-254) helpfully summed up the three-fold nature of the debt we owe.[6] First, the debt we owe to our fellow humans: to parents, to children, to strangers, to the poor, to the aged, to those in authority; to love our neighbor as we love our self; to love one another as Jesus loves us.

Second, the debt we owe to ourselves: to our body, not to abuse it, to care for it as God's temple; to our mind, to use it in such a way that it gets sharper as we grow; to our soul, to watch over it so that we live in holiness and vitality.

Third, the debt we owe to God: to love God with all our heart and soul and mind and strength; to trust God with all our needs and worries. While we are alive, says Origen, "there is not a single hour, day or night," when we are "not a debtor."[7]

Do you see then why I said that the fifth petition of the Lord's Prayer is the *boldest* prayer a human being can pray? "Father in heaven, Creator and Judge, forgive us our debts, cancel our debts, all of them. The debts owed to others, the debts owed to ourselves, the debts owed to you. Cancel them all!"

And—wonder of all wonders—he cancels all the debt.

Psalm 32, verse 5, says

> I acknowledged my sin to you
> and did not cover up my iniquity.
> I said, "I will confess
> my transgressions to the LORD."
> And you forgave
> the guilt of my sin.

Psalm 103, verses 10-12, says

> He does not treat us as our sins deserve
> or repay us according to our iniquities.
> For as high as the heavens are above the earth,
> so great is his love for those who fear him;

as far as the east is from the west,
so far has he removed our transgressions from us.

"Just like that?" you might ask. "We ask the Father of the Lord Jesus to forgive our debts, and just like that he does?"

Yes, just like that.

"But it cannot be that simple, can it? I mean, what about justice? What about orderliness? If banks forgave debt like that there would be utter chaos. Can you imagine walking into your bank and asking the teller to cancel the mortgage?"

Well, yes, I can imagine that. I imagine it regularly. But I cannot imagine any human banker honoring my request.

This is the good news. The apostle Paul uses the language of the fifth petition of the Lord's Prayer when he writes to the Colossians:

> And when you were dead in your transgressions and the uncircumcison of your flesh, God made you alive together with Christ, having forgiven us all our transgressions, having canceled out the certificate of debt consisting of decrees against us and which were hostile to us; and he has taken it out of the way, having nailed it to the cross. (Colossians 2:13-14)

What a liberating picture! The list of decrees against us, all the particulars of the titanic mortgage upon our lives—that long, long list of failures to do our duties. That long, long, long list of debts—Jesus Christ has grabbed hold of it all and taken it to the cross. And by his blood he has canceled it all! The one who teaches us to pray so boldly, "Father, forgive us our debts," is the one who takes our debts upon himself, goes to the cross and dies to erase the ledger.

J. B. Phillips rendered Paul's words this way: "Christ has utterly wiped out the damning evidence of broken laws and commandments which always hung over our heads, and has completely annulled it by nailing it over his own head on the cross."[8] The boldest prayer we can pray is answered because the one who teaches us to pray pays the debt himself—all of it. Whatever it is we owe, Jesus Christ has paid it all. As one writer has phrased it, "He came to pay a debt he did not owe, because we owed a debt we cannot pay."[9]

> My sin—O the joy of this glorious thought
> My sin, not in part, but the whole,
> Is nailed to the cross, and I bear it no more:
> Praise the Lord, praise the Lord, O my soul.[10]

"As we also have forgiven our debtors." *As.* What does Jesus mean? What is the meaning of the "as"? "As we also have forgiven our debtors?" Is it "because?" "Cancel our debts *because* we have canceled the debt of others?" Is it "to the degree?" "Cancel our debts *to the degree* we have canceled the debts of others?" Horrifying thought! Is it "simultaneously?" "Cancel our debts as we now are *in the process* of canceling the debts of others?" In his elaboration on the fifth petition, Jesus seems to make our being forgiven contingent upon our forgiving others. Is Rabbi Gamaliel, at whose feet the apostle Paul studied before meeting Jesus, right when he says, "So long as you are merciful, God will have mercy upon you, and if you are not merciful, he will not be merciful to you?"[11]

Martin Luther took it on face value that there is a one-to-one correspondence between our forgiving others and our being forgiven by God. So much so that he argued if I do not forgive others I am actually praying, "Father, do not forgive me." What? Luther works with Psalm 109:7: "Let his prayer be counted as sin!" He writes,

> Psalm 109:7 says his prayer will be a sin in the sight of God; for what else can you mean when you say, "I will not forgive," and yet

stand before God and pray, "Forgive us our debts, as we forgive our debtors." What else can you mean than this; "Oh God, I am your debtor, and I also have a debtor; I am not willing to forgive him, therefore do not forgive me. I will not obey you though you should declare me pardoned; I would rather renounce your heaven and everything else, and go to the devil"?[12]

Is Luther right—that not forgiving others is actually asking God not to forgive me?

The way I understand what Jesus is teaching us is this: if I am not willing to forgive others then I am not asking God to forgive me, no matter what words I use. I am asking God to excuse me, but not asking God to forgive me.

Let me elaborate. There are three interrelated words involved in any act of forgiveness. They are justice, mercy, and grace.[13] Justice is God giving me what I deserve. Mercy is God not giving me what I deserve. Grace is God giving me what I do not deserve.

When I authentically pray, "Father, forgive me my debts," I am asking God not to exercise justice, right? *Oh Father, you have every right to give me what I deserve—judgment—but I am asking you not to do it.* Instead, I am asking God to exercise mercy. "O Father, do not give me what I deserve." And I am asking God to grant me grace. "O Father, not only do not give me what I deserve, give me what I do not deserve, give me life with you!"

Now, what is going on in my heart when I refuse to forgive others? I am demanding that justice be done. "That person hurt me deeply and deserves justice." I am not wanting the other person to experience mercy. "That person should be punished or be made to pay the debt." And I am certainly not extending grace. "That person should have to go on in her or his misery until the debt is paid."

Are those two movements of the heart compatible? Can the human heart stand before God in those two very different modes? No. It is like saying, "Father, I take my stand before you on the basis of the cross of Christ, but she cannot. She cannot benefit from the cross. She must stand before you on her own merit. She has to pay up first." To say that reveals that I have no clue of what it means to pray the Lord's Prayer. Although I am mouthing the words "forgive me my debts," I am not meaning what I am saying. If I will not cancel your indebtedness to me I cannot possibly be asking God to cancel my indebtedness to him. I must be thinking that somehow my debt is not that big a deal or I have some excuse that justifies me not living up to my duty. I am in no way praying the Prayer.

The British preacher John Stott expresses it best: "God forgives only the penitent, and one of the chief evidences of true penitence is a forgiving spirit."[14] The servant in Jesus' parable had no clue of what the master had done for him. He had canceled an enormous debt—ten million dollars!—which he could never have paid back, and then the servant could not cancel the minor debt of a slave. He totally missed what was going on. He totally missed the interplay between justice, mercy and grace.

Yes, forgiving those who have sinned against us is not easy. It is hard work, costly work, painful work. The greater the sin, the harder the work of forgiving. Just as it takes time for us to experience the Father's forgiveness of us, so it takes time to really experience letting go of the sin of others against us. But let it go we must. For it turns out that the person who suffers the most when we will not forgive is ourself. Christian ethicist Lewis Smedes writes, "To forgive is to set a prisoner free." Isn't that good? "To forgive is to set a prisoner free, *and discover that the prisoner is you*."[15] If we will decide, as an act of our will, to forgive, God will give us grace to do it—and we will be free.

"As we also have forgiven our debtors." We forgive? We? As the Pharisees rightly asked Jesus, "Who can forgive sins but God alone?" (Mark 2:7). And so many others throughout church history have said that we are never more like God than when we forgive.[16]

"Father in heaven, forgive us our debts, as we also have forgiven our debtors."

Allow me to now lead you in a "debt cancellation" exercise. I invite you to bring to mind the person you are having a hard time forgiving. I invite you to tell the Father the person's name. And I invite you to tell the Father exactly what this person did to you. Be honest, specific, and ruthless.

Now tell the Father what you would like to see happen to this person. Do not be afraid, he knows what is in your heart even if you do not tell him. Tell him how you want to see this person punished or shamed or hurt as you were hurt.

Now imagine standing at the bottom of a hill. On top of the hill is a cross. Jesus is hanging there. He invites you to come up the hill. What do you want to say to him? More of what you have already told the Father? Look into his eyes. Tell him how hard it is to forgive.

And now, as an act of your will, go back down the hill and invite the person who hurt you to come back up the hill with you. Bring the person to the foot of the cross. Looking at Jesus, and pointing to that person, as an act of your will say, "Jesus, grant this person what you have granted me."

And hear Jesus say, "I will. Blessed are you. You are never more like me and my Father than when you forgive. Go in peace."

7

RESCUE US!

Deliver us from the evil one.

artin Luther is reputed to have said that he went to bed with the fifth petition of the Lord's Prayer and woke up with the sixth. It makes sense, does it not? We go to bed reviewing the day and realize we need to pray the fifth petition, "forgive us our debts, as we have forgiven our debtors." We wake up previewing the day, and realize we need to pray the sixth petition, "lead us not into temptation, but deliver us from the evil one."

Not just "deliver us from evil," although it is not wrong to pray that way. It's just that in the sixth petition Jesus uses the definite article: *"the* evil." He uses this same phrase in the rest of his Sermon on the Mount (Matt 5:37) to refer to his enemy, the devil, "the evil one." He is the one who has rebelled against God: the one who seeks to dishonor the name of the Father; the one who seeks to deprive the Father's children of daily bread; the one who seeks to divide the Father's children from him and from each other by causing them to cling to their hurts and grievances.

This sixth petition is at once the most critical petition for us to pray and yet the most puzzling. The difficulty is this: why ask God not to do what is not in the character of God to do? Would the God we meet in Jesus ever intentionally lead us into temptation? Then why bother praying, "Lead us not?"

TEMPTATION?

The word translated "temptation" is the Greek word *peirasmos*, which has two different meanings. One is "test"; the other is "temptation." These are two very different things! A test is something meant to prove a person's character and, in the process, improve it. A temptation is meant to entice a person to sin, to bring a person down in some way. A *peirasmos* is a difficult or challenging situation in life, which can either be a test, proving and improving a person's character, or a temptation, enticing a person into the way of sin. Whether it is a test or a temptation depends on who is behind it and how we respond.

Hence the puzzling wording of the sixth petition of the Lord's Prayer. If God does not tempt anyone, why pray "lead us not into temptation"? That is, why bother asking God not to do what God would never do? Are we not wasting our breath?

Can this difficulty be resolved? Yes. By paying attention to the whole petition. The prayer is not just, "lead us not into temptation." The prayer is, "lead us not into temptation, *but* deliver us from the evil one." The little word "but" ties the two clauses together. How? The second clause interprets the first clause. "But deliver us from the evil one" interprets "lead us not into temptation."

And what is the interpretation? It is this: the evil one seeks to *turn* tests into *temptations*! In this petition Jesus reveals one of the most fundamental truths of life. Jesus' enemy turns tests into temptations. There are events or experiences in life through which the Father intends to prove and improve our character and faith, but the evil one sneaks in and intends to destroy our character and faith. It is very subtle and unrelenting. What the Father of Jesus means as a test, the evil one seeks to turn into a temptation.

How then should we word the sixth petition of the Lord's Prayer? What is Jesus teaching us to pray? I think it is this: "Father, as you lead us into the test, do not let the test become a temptation, but deliver us from the evil one." Or, "Father, you know that we cannot stand up under very much pressure. As you lead us to the test—all of life is a test!—as you seek to prove and improve our faith, do not let the test become a temptation, a seduction to sin, but deliver us from the subtle wiles of the deceiver against whom we are no match. Father, rescue us from the evil one!"

WHY TEST?

Let us go deeper and ask why God tests us. God does not tempt anyone, but he does test everyone. Why does God test us? For one basic reason. Life with a capital 'L' is found in trusting God. Do you agree? Indeed, life with a capital 'L' is found only in trusting God. The quality of Life is, therefore, a function of the quality of our trust. So, to make sure our trust is, in fact, in God and God alone, God puts us to the test. The word *peirasmos*, says New Testament scholar William Barclay, "is regularly used of the divine placing of a man in a situation which is a test, a situation in which he may fall, but in which he is not meant to fall, a situation which may be his ruin, but out of which he is meant to emerge spiritually strengthened and enriched."

The word *peirasmos* is used of the process of refining gold. A goldsmith takes a piece of ore from the ground, both to reveal and to refine. To reveal that it really is gold, and to refine it into pure gold, so God does with us. God puts us to the test to reveal and to refine, to reveal whether we are trusting God or not and to refine our trust in him. Just about every event or experience in life serves as a test! The very situation intended by "Our Father" for good, the evil one seeks to turn for bad. He seeks to turn the Father's *peirasmos* from a test into a temptation.

How does the evil one attempt this? Why would the evil one even bother? Because he does not like the Father of the Lord Jesus. That is putting it mildly. He does not like Jesus. That is an understatement. He does not want anyone to like Jesus and his Father. He does not want anyone to trust Jesus and his Father. And so he seeks to get us to doubt the goodness of God. That is his major goal. Yes, he seeks to engender violence and hostility and addiction. Yes, he seeks to wreak all kinds of havoc and chaos. But his one major goal is to get us to doubt that Jesus' Father is good and faithful. Once he has done that, the rest is easy.

We see this at work in the two major temptation stories in the Bible, or as I should put it, in the two major "testing-being-made-temptation" stories in the Bible. Genesis 3, where the first Adam and Eve faced the subtlety and failed, and Matthew 4, where Jesus, the second Adam, faced the subtleties and won.

STRATEGIES OF THE EVIL ONE

In these two stories we discover five strategies Satan uses to turn a test into a temptation.

Strategy one: *sow seeds of suspicion.* The evil one begins by raising suspicion that the Living God is not wholly disposed toward our good. In the Genesis story he does this by conveniently leaving out key words of God's command. He says to Eve, "Has God said, 'You must not eat from any tree in the garden'?" (Gen 3:1). Is that what God said? No. God said, "You are free to eat from any tree in the garden; but you must not eat from the tree of the knowledge of good and evil" (Gen 2:16-17). See what the evil one has done? He has turned God's positive into a negative. God said, "You are free to eat from any tree;" the evil one says, "You shall not eat from any tree." And he left out the word "free."[1]

When Eve quotes God's words back to the evil one, she, having begun to become suspicious of God, leaves out "free," and says we are not to eat or "touch" the tree of knowledge of good and evil, and says that it is "in the middle." Not so. The tree of life is in the middle, not the tree of the knowledge of good and evil. She "moves it" to the middle, making it problematic.[2] The implication being she is becoming suspicious that God is withholding something she and Adam need in order to be fully human.

I often experience this twisting of God's word in the direction of suspicion. For example, in Luke 12:32, "Do not be afraid, little flock, the Father has chosen to give you the kingdom." Is that what Jesus says? No. I keep forgetting two key words, "your" and "gladly." "Do not be afraid, little flock, *your* Father has chosen *gladly* to give you the kingdom" (NASB).

Matthew 6:33: "Seek first his kingdom and righteousness; and these things will be added to you." Is that what Jesus says? No. I keep forgetting the key word "all." "Seek first his kingdom and righteousness; and *all* these things will be added to you." I keep forgetting little words like "your," "gladly," and "all," because someone wants me to forget them. Someone wants me to think that the Living God is holding back, that he is not generously disposed toward me.

Strategy two: *focus on the negative.* The evil one seeks to get us to focus on the negative circumstances of our lives. In the desert, in the Matthew story, the evil one comes to Jesus and says, "If you are the Son of God, tell these stones to become bread" (4:3). "Stones, Jesus. Stones. Just stones. That's all there is out here, Jesus. Stones. Hot, hard stones. No trees. No grass. No water. No sagebrush. Just stones. Nothing but stones. Pretty barren, Jesus. Just stones." Ever heard that in your head? All the time? Someone has said that Satan is the original "negative thinker," always focusing on the negative.

Strategy three: *make deductions from the negative.* The evil one seeks to help us make deductions from the negative circumstances—false deductions. Again, in the desert, in the Matthew story, he says to Jesus, "If you are the Son of God, tell these stones to become bread." "If you are." The evil one is not questioning the fact, nor getting Jesus to question it. That would not have worked. The evil one is simply raising a question about the quality of Jesus' relationship with his Father.[3]

"Son, *huh? The* Son. *The* Beloved *Son, as the voice said at your baptism. I don't want to be disrespectful Jesus, but these are pretty crummy circumstances for the Son of the Father. I mean, it seems to me that if you are the Son of God, if the Father loves you as he claimed at your baptism, he would not let this happen to you. It seems to me, Jesus, that you have been deserted."*

Have you ever heard that in your head? The evil one, first getting us to focus on the negative dimensions of our broken circumstances, then wants us to conclude we are in this difficult place because the Father does not care as much as Jesus says he does. Why would a child of God ever be in a desert-kind of place?

We may think the Father must have let us down, not realizing that the desert just may be the place of great redemption. It may be the place where having been stripped of all that is not God we are left with God alone, and are, therefore, in a most blessed state.

Sow suspicion. Focus on the negative. Make false deductions about the quality of our relationship with the Father. And then strategy four: *force the Father's hand.*

"The Father does not seem to be doing anything about your circumstances, Jesus. Why not throw his words at him, Jesus? Stand on the pinnacle of the temple, and throw yourself off the edge. Jesus, here is God's word, Psalm 91:11-12—'He will give his angels charge concerning you' and 'On their hands they will bear you up, lest you strike your foot against the stone.' Jesus, are you listening to me? Something is wrong with your circumstances. The Father seems so passive, so inactive. Do this Jesus. Say to your Father, who claims to love you, 'You said you will send angels to keep me from hurting myself. So here I go. I am going to jump and give you an opportunity to prove your love for me. If you love me you will catch me.'"

The evil one is always suggesting to us ways we can get God to prove his love. But it never works. For one thing God will not play the game. For another, if God did what we suggested we would not be satisfied. It would not prove his love. It would mean God is not God because he, like us, can be manipulated.

So since God does not play the game, strategy five: *take things into our own hands.* The evil one seeks to get us to *take* our lives into our own hands.

"Look Jesus, I am only here to help you. Since God has abandoned you out here—and I am really sorry about that—and since he does not seem to be lifting a finger to help you—and I am

really sorry about that too—you simply need to take things into your own hands. See all the kingdoms of the world? See all their glory? They are supposed to be given to you. Psalm 2— "The nations of the world are to be given to the Beloved Son. Well, I have an offer for you. Fall down and worship me and they are all yours. I will give them all to you. I will release my grip and they will be yours. You can avoid the ridiculously naive plan of your Father whereby you win the nations by dying for the sin of the world. Now *Jesus, you can have it all now, without all that suffering. No one needs to know what you have done. I'll let it be our little secret. Here, out in the desert where no one sees, you bow down and worship me just for a moment and everything is yours. Jesus, does it matter how you get what you want just so long as you get it? Does it matter what means you use as long as you get the desired end?"*

Have you ever heard anything like that in your head? Once the seeds of suspicion have been sown and begin to grow; once we begin to dwell on the negative dimensions of life and begin to deduce that something is wrong between us and the Father; once we have tried to force God's hand and found it does not work, we are vulnerable to the subtle push to take charge of our lives and meet our needs anyway we can. And thus, we end up no longer trusting God, and no longer experiencing life with a capital *L*.

That is why Jesus teaches us to pray, *"Our Father, we cannot stand up under very much pressure. We are not wise enough to recognize and then counter the work of the evil one. When you lead us to the test, when life itself brings us to the test, do not let the test become a temptation, but rescue us. Rescue us from the subtle strategies of the evil one, and help us trust you."*

This prayer God is more than pleased to answer. My wife Sharon and I are testimonies to his answering it. Four days before Christmas of 2000 our then 18-year-old son Alex, whom we had adopted six years earlier from an orphanage in Moscow, went hiking with a group of friends in the mountains just north of Los Angeles. They were making their way along a loose rock slope when the rocks gave way, and Alex slid down the slope and then over a 120-foot cliff. When the rescue team arrived some 40 minutes later, the helicopter pilot said he was sure Alex was dead—too much blood had flowed from his head for him to be alive. But when two of the paramedics got to him they found a pulse, and quickly rushed him to the trauma center in Pasadena. By the time Sharon and I made it to the hospital, Alex was already in a coma and attached to life-support systems. The neurosurgeons could not say whether Alex would live. If he made it until Christmas Eve then there was hope he would recover. Even if he survived, the doctors would not say what kind of life he would have.

On the night before Christmas Eve, as I drove home from having spent the day in the ICU, I heard the following words, which I keep in my journal:

> Things are not as they seem. In your life. In your son's life. In your wife's life. In the lives of your other children. In the lives of other patients in ICU. Things are not as they seem. There is more going on than meets the un-aided senses. There is a God. A Living God. A good God. A faithful God. A powerful God. A reigning God. An ever-present God. There is never a time when this God is not good. There is never a time when this God is not faithful. There is never a time when this God is not powerful. There is never a time when the God of the Bible is not on the throne of the universe. There is never a time when the God we meet in Jesus is not present. It is a promise: "I will never leave you or forsake you."

"Things are not as they seem." In one of the most frightening experiences of our lives, our heavenly Father rescued us from the evil one's attempt to destroy our faith.

(Alex, I am grateful to report, lived and is making a remarkable recovery. And he loves the Father. *That* is the miracle).

"Our Father in heaven, as you lead us to the test, do not let the test become a temptation, but rescue us from the one who seeks to destroy our faith and work in us the same confidence in you that Jesus has. Amen."

NOT ALL THAT COMPLICATED

What a gift! These fifty-seven words (in the Greek text anyway) we call "the Lord's Prayer" are one of the greatest gifts he could give us. After making our way through the Prayer one line at a time, wouldn't you agree?

I first began to realize just how wonderful a gift the Lord's Prayer is in June of 1984. Sharon and I were living in Los Angeles, where I was serving as the Pastor of St. John's Presbyterian Church. The church's buildings were located just north of Los Angeles International Airport and just south of the campus of the University of California at Los Angeles. The church was growing both numerically and spiritually. It was thrilling to be part of such a vital work of the Holy Spirit! Yet I was restless in my spirit. I was longing for more, for more of God. I felt a great need to go deeper in prayer.

Providentially, an opportunity to go to Korea came my way. I had been hearing about what the Holy Spirit was doing in and through the church in Korea; in particular, hearing about the role prayer was playing. By 1984 the prayer-life of Korean Christians was becoming well known all over the world. So when the opportunity arose to travel to Korea it felt like an answer to my longing.

The Lausanne Committee on World Evangelization was inviting Christian leaders from all over the world to join together in Seoul, South Korea, for what they were calling the International Prayer Assembly. It was the first time in world history that Christians from all over the globe and from every denominational affiliation would meet for the expressed purpose of simply praying for the evangelization of the world. In June of 1984 we met at Yang Nak Presbyterian Church in the heart of Seoul. Yang Nak was, and still is, the largest Presbyterian Church in the world. In 1984 its membership was 90,000!

I can still remember the opening worship service of the Prayer Assembly. As we sang the hymn "All Hail the Power of Jesus' Name" (which I'm told was the most-sung hymn of the twentieth century) representatives from 76 different countries of the world brought their nations' flags to the front of the sanctuary. What a powerful sign of the fact that world evangelization has in fact been happening, and what a sign of hope that it will continue to happen. Just before singing the last verse of the hymn, the worship leader invited us to sing it in our native languages. I can still hear the sound, a foretaste of heaven as in seventy different languages we sang,

> Oh that with yonder sacred throng,
> We at his feet may fall,
> We'll join the everlasting song,
> And crown Him Lord of all.

Each day of the assembly we would meet to pray, receive teaching on prayer, pray, receive more teaching, pray, and receive yet more teaching. Morning to evening, every day. Very stretching. But as the days went by, I was becoming more and more uncomfortable. *Troubled* would be a better word. It felt to me that things were getting too complicated. I was feeling more and more overwhelmed. We were receiving teaching on how to pray for various parts of the world, and on how to pray for the various cultural and political dynamics of the various parts of the world. We heard about how to pray when "such and such" is the case, how to pray when another "such and such" is the case, how to pray when yet another "such and such" is the case. We were not hearing this from the Koreans. They simply prayed! We were hearing this from the non-Koreans, from Western Christians in particular, who, as we Westerners tend to do, were analyzing what the Koreans were doing and were trying to find a way to systematize it all, "to package it," and make it all into some kind of "program." I found myself not wanting to enter into prayer times. Was I too fatigued, I wondered? Was I too proud or, worse yet, did I have a hardened heart toward God?

Toward the end of the assembly we were given the opportunity to spend a day at a "Prayer Mountain." You may know that many of the Korean congregations have built conference centers along the DMZ (De-Militarized-Zone) that divides North and South Korea. Most Korean disciples at that time spent one of their two weeks of vacation fasting and praying at a Prayer Mountain. They met together in very large auditoriums, five to ten thousand at a time, or prayed alone in little bunkers or caves built into the hills around the conference centers.

As we traveled in the bus north of Seoul, the uneasiness nagged at me. Why was I troubled? Why was I feeling overwhelmed?

When we arrived at the Prayer Mountain I hoped to be able to spend time in one of the bunkers. Since I could see only about 100 bunkers, and since we participants numbered about 2,500, I was prepared not to get my wish. But as I walked around the bunker-area, an elderly Korean man came out of his "prayer closet," telling me in broken English that he needed to attend to something else for a while, and inviting me to use his "cave" while he was gone.

I entered the four-foot high, three-foot wide space with all kinds of feelings. On the one hand, joyful gratitude; on the other, that nagging uneasiness. As soon as I entered the space I felt that the only appropriate thing to do was to kneel. So I did. And before I could do anything else, I was bent over, my face on the ground, weeping. All I could do was weep. The sense of God's presence was palpable. As I wept I felt the Lord speak to me. I did not hear a voice, but I did hear in my head the words, "It is not that complicated." And I sensed I was to open my Bible to Matthew 6, to the Lord's Prayer. As I read those fifty-seven words, I had the distinct impression that God was saying, "Do not complicate the act of prayer—it is so much more straightforward than my people make it out to be." I have sought to live in and from the Lord's Prayer ever since.

Oh what a gift! Jesus is absolutely brilliant. His little Prayer covers everything any human, any where, any time, needs to pray.

Let me now review what we have discovered as we have been unwrapping the gift in this book.

(1) In his prayer Jesus gives us the gift of *identity*. The gift of a new identity. We are children. We are daughters and sons of a heavenly Father. No other act in life reinforces this as does the act of praying the Lord's Prayer, for we pray it as children. We are not just creatures of the Creator. We are not just servants of

the Master. We are children loved by a Father. The first word of the prayer is "Father." In English the first word is "our." But in the original the first word is "Father." *Pater* in Greek. *Abba* in Aramaic. "Daddy" in English. Jesus teaches us to address the Holy, Sovereign God of the Universe as "Father." That is, Jesus teaches us to address the Holy sovereign of the universe the same way he does. Others in Jesus' day were praying "Holy One," or "Almighty," or "Rock," or "Lord of Hosts." Jesus was praying "Father." It is the word we hear on the lips of Jesus again and again. In the beginning of his earthly life—"did you not know that I had to be in my Father's house?" (Luke 2:49, NASB). In the end—"*Father*, into your hands I commit my spirit" (Luke 23:46). And at every point along the way, he is saying the same: "I only do what I see my Father doing, I only say what I hear my Father saying" (see John 5:19-20). Jesus is self-consciously the Son, the Son of God the Father. His whole identity is as "Son of the Father." It is into that same identity that Jesus brings us. "Come, follow me," he says. "Where are we going?" we ask. "Into the same relationship I have with the Father." We are, as one New Testament scholar has recently put it, "enfranchised into Jesus' status" as the Beloved.[1] We now get to enter into and enjoy the same kind of relationship Jesus has with his Father. Like Jesus, we too are now sons and daughters of God!

(2) In his prayer, Jesus gives us the gift of *access*—access to headquarters. "Our Father in heaven." "In heaven" is a way of saying "on the throne" (see Matthew 5:34). We have access to the throne, to the throne of the universe—the *same* access Jesus has! Have you ever tried to gain access to someone who has more authority than you? It's not easy. Try getting an audience this afternoon with the Queen of England. Or try getting an audience with the President of the United States. Or with your

favorite celebrity. What are the odds? Not very good unless you know someone who has access. Or unless you are related to them in some way, or better yet, unless you are one of their children.

Jesus has given us access to the throne of the universe. He can give it because he has it all of the time. He has always had it, always will have it, and he gives it to us. "Just tell the throne, 'Jesus sent me.'" Imagine that: we can walk into the headquarters of the universe and say to the one who sits on the throne, "Father," and he receives us and hears us. "Through him," says the apostle Paul, "we have access to the Father" (Eph 2:18). No paperwork. No security checks. No admission fees. Just walk into the throne-room and say, "Father, I am here because of Jesus." He welcomes us with open arms.

(3) In his prayer Jesus gives us the gift of *revelation*—revelation of who the Father is and what the Father is like. The Lord's Prayer reveals more of the nature and character of the Father than any other words of Jesus. In his Prayer, Jesus reveals his own understanding of the Father.

"Father in heaven," Jesus called him. In our day "heaven" refers to a place and time far, far away, disconnected from and unrelated to earth. Not in Jesus' day; not in the Bible. For Jesus "heaven" is another dimension of reality very close at hand, both in terms of place and time. "Heaven" is another dimension of reality that sustains all the dimensions of reality we can see and hear and touch. "Heaven" is another dimension of reality that intersects and permeates all of the other dimensions of reality. Heaven is all around us. "Father in heaven" is a way of saying, "Father very close at hand."

Each of the petitions of the prayer then reveals something of the Father. "Your name be hallowed." It says the Father cares about his honor, his reputation. It says the Father will always act in ways that are consistent with his character (see Luke 11:5-8). "Your kingdom come." It says the Father is not just a parent, but is also a King, the King, the King of Kings. It says the Father is active in the world setting up his rule and overcoming all that gets in the way of his rule. "Your will be done." It says the Father has a plan—a good plan, a perfect plan—and he is at work fulfilling it. "Give us this day our daily bread." It says the Father cares about the concrete needs of flesh and blood people. It says the Father is a Provider. "Cancel our debts as we cancel the debts of others" says the Father is a Reconciler and Forgiver. It says the Father wants relationships to work, and is at work to tear down the barriers. It says the Father is the Liberator, breaking the yoke of indebtedness. "As you lead us to the test, do not let the test become a temptation, but rescue us from the evil one." It says that the Father knows where we live, in a battlefield, where the enemy of Jesus seeks to ruin us. It says the Father seeks to prove and improve our faith, and will protect us from the one who wants to destroy our faith. In his Prayer, Jesus reveals what he knows about the Father.

(4) In his Prayer Jesus gives us the gift of *relief*. That is the best way I know how to put it. He gives us relief from the burden of wondering if what we are praying is right to pray. For years I struggled with fearing that my prayers were too selfish and too idealistic. What a relief the Lord's Prayer gives! Jesus has been showing me that my prayers are not too selfish or too idealistic. He is showing us that they are not selfish enough, they are not idealistic enough! "Here is what to pray," he says, "Your desires are not great enough. Pray like this."

"Your name be hallowed." Ask the Father to make his name known, ask him to manifest his character to you and to the world, so that the whole earth is filled with the knowledge of the Lord as the water covers the seas. Top that in your idealism! Father, let us know you to the degree Jesus knows you!

"Your kingdom come." Ask the Father to establish his reign in the world so that he, and he alone, rules the nations of the earth. Ask the Father to bring in a whole new world order, to affect the ultimate and final "regime change," so that justice and grace and healing and peace flow like a river. Top that in your idealism! "Father, rule without rival in every corner of this globe!"

"Your will be done." Ask the Father to fulfill all his good-pleasures, so that the reason he even bothered to create the earth, and create us, might come to full realization. Ask the Father to cause humanity to truly live as the "image of God," to live as creatures filled with the life of God. Top that in your idealism, Darrell! Ask the Father to recapitulate the human race, to put the Head back on the race.

"Give us this day our daily bread." Ask the Father for everything you need in order to be all he calls you to be. Ask him for bread, yes, and for wisdom and strength and grace. Ask him to provide the resources you need in order to serve him with excellence and joy. Ask him to so work in the world that no one is ever hungry! Top that in your selfishness!

"Cancel our debts as we cancel the debts of others." Incredible. "The whole list, Father, the list of all my debts against you and others, the whole lot, cancel it." And he does! Top that in your selfishness!

"As you lead us to the test, do not let the test become a temptation, but rescue us from the evil one." Really? I can really ask for this? This pleases God? Asking him to keep my faith alive under the pressure we face in a broken world? I can ask the Father to give me what I need in order to even ask the Father? I can ask for *faith*? And ask for my faith to be *made* strong? What a relief!

(5) In his Prayer Jesus gives us the gift of *vision*. In his prayer he is giving us his vision of the Christian life. As we observed in the first chapter, here we have a pattern for discipleship. *Name*: we come to know the character of God. *Kingdom*: we come to know how God works and reigns in the world, and how we co-operate with him. *Will*: we come to know what God desires, and how he is fulfilling his good pleasures in us. *Bread*: we come to know how God provides for the disciples of Jesus, learning how to trust him one day at a time. *Forgiveness*: we come into the reconciliation God has worked out in Jesus' death, and learn how to live in reconciliation. *Temptation/evil one*: we learn how to deal with spiritual opposition, learning how to stand in the victory of Jesus. And then *name* again: getting to know the character of God even more fully.

(6) In his Prayer Jesus gives us the gift of *meaning*. Our lives are given greater meaning for we are brought in on the mystery of God's way in the world: that the Father chooses to work in the world through the prayers of his children. We are given what Blaise Pascal called "the dignity of causality." In praying we are participating in God fulfilling his purposes in the world. We also do so in our preaching, teaching, counseling and serving, but chiefly through our praying.

Would the Father do all Jesus teaches us to ask him even if we did not pray? On the one hand, yes. No one prayed for creation to happen. No one was there to ask. No one prayed for the incarnation to happen, for God to come to earth as one of us, to take on our flesh. No one even thought of such a radical act. So, yes, God would still do what Jesus says he desires to do even if we did not pray. God would still hallow his name, and bring in his kingdom, and accomplish his will, even if no one prayed. But, on the other hand, no, he would not do it if we did not pray, for he has chosen to do what he could freely do in response to our prayers. Thus we have the dignity of causality. It is all unleashed, if you will, as we pray. Some say it is mere coincidence that kingdom kinds of things happen when we pray. Maybe so. But as William Temple, then Archbishop of Canterbury, once said, "When I pray, coincidences happen; when I stop praying, the coincidences stop happening." It turns out that the movers and shakers of history are those who pray the Lord's Prayer. The real movers and shakers are those who go into the headquarters and move the one who moves and shakes history.

(7) In his Prayer Jesus give us the gift of *boldness*. Again, that is the only way I know how to put it at this point in my understanding. He has given us boldness in our access. The verbs in all six petitions are in the imperative mood: they are commands! The first three verbs—*hallow, come, be*—are in the passive voice. This is partially to mute the audacity of the imperative, but mostly to emphasize that only God can do what is being requested. The way to render the petitions to capture these nuances of grammar is this: "Only you can hallow your name, so do it." "Only you can cause your kingdom to come, so do it." "Only you can make your will be done, so do it." "Only you can provide us with our daily bread, so do it." "Only you can cancel our debts, so do it." "Only you can keep us from the evil one in times of test, so do it."

Jesus is teaching us the amazing truth that we, as his adopted brothers and sisters, can walk into the headquarters of the universe (through prayer) and entreat the Sovereign God that boldly! It pleases God to be so entreated, though I, for one, am not yet comfortable with this boldness—I feel I need to insert the word, "please." "Only you can hallow your name, so please do it Father." "Only you can cancel our debts, so please do it Father."

That is bold enough! But Jesus has given us freedom to exercise even greater boldness.

"*Only you* can do it." Again, in this prayer we are asking God to do what only God can do. We are not praying, "Let *us* hallow your name, let *us* bring in your kingdom, let *us* do your will," although it is perfectly acceptable to pray that way. What we are praying is, "*You* hallow your name, because *only* you can. *You* bring in your kingdom, because *only* you can. *You* provide us all we need, because *only* you can."

"And you can! You can do it, Father." That is the point of the conclusion to the prayer that was added after Matthew published his Gospel: "For yours is the kingdom, and the power, and the glory, forever. Amen." The church rightly did not want to end with, "But deliver us from the evil-one."[2] It was inconceivable to the church that, "within the Jewish praying styles of his day," Jesus would not end without a final statement of why the prayer can be answered.[3] King David ended his prayer at the coronation of King Solomon (1 Chr 29:11) with these words:

Yours, LORD, is the greatness and the power
and the glory and the majesty and the splendor,
for everything in heaven and earth is yours.
Yours, LORD, is the kingdom;
you are exalted as head over all.

So the early church believed that David's greater Son, King Jesus, ended his prayer, "For yours is the kingdom and the power, and the glory, forever." ("For," meaning, "all we have asked you to do you can do.")

"*For the kingdom is yours: you are sovereign over all, always have been, always will be. You can do whatever you choose to do. You can do it for the power is yours: all power, power to do whatever you choose to do. You made the world out of nothing;*

you raised Jesus from the dead. You have the power to fulfill your will, to provide us all we need, and overcome the evil-one. And you can do it for yours is the glory. Glory stands for all that makes you be you, all that makes you the Sovereign, powerful God you are. Infinite resources are yours. You can do all and more than we can ever dare to imagine! Only you, Father, can do all this. And you have what it takes to do what only you can do.

(8) And finally (for now), in his prayer Jesus gives us the gift of *himself.* For as we have seen throughout our journey in the Lord's Prayer, it turns out that Jesus himself is the answer to each petition of the Prayer. All six petitions of the Lord's Prayer will be answered because the Lord who teaches us to pray is *himself* the answer.

"Your name be hallowed," and *Jesus shows up*, the perfect revelation and manifestation of the Father's character.

"Your kingdom come," and *Jesus shows up*, the full embodiment of the reign of the Father.

"Your will be done," and *Jesus shows up*, living out the Father's good pleasures in our flesh and blood.

"Give us this day our daily bread," and *Jesus shows up*, as the Bread of Life, who alone can satisfy the ravenous hunger of the human soul.

"Cancel our debts," and *Jesus shows up*, taking up our debts and erasing them by his blood, paying the debt himself, empowering us to cancel the debts of others.

"Rescue us from the evil-one," and *Jesus shows up*, overcoming the tempter's subtle schemes, disarming him through death on the cross.

The apostle Paul says of Jesus that he is the "yes" to all of God's promises (2 Cor 1:20). And it turns out that he is the "yes" to all our prayers. The answer to the Lord's Prayer is as sure as the Lord himself.

Again, what a gift! And not that complicated at all. Fifty-seven words that put everything into perspective. Fifty-seven words that change the world by bringing the reality of heaven down to earth.

Our Father,
very close at hand,
on the throne of the universe:
Be hallowed (!) your name,
on earth as it is in heaven;
Come (!) your kingdom,
on earth as it is in heaven;
Be done (!) your will,
on earth as it is in heaven.
Give us this day all we need to be your people.
Cancel our debts,
as we have cancelled the debts of our debtors.
And as you lead us to the test,
do not let the test become a temptation,
but rescue us from the twisting wiles of the evil-one.
(He wants us to think that
    you are not as good as Jesus says you are.)
All this, and more, you can do,
for yours is the kingdom,
and the power
and the glory.
Forever!
So be it.

NOTES

CHAPTER 1: BRINGING HEAVEN DOWN

1. Blaise Pascal, *Pensées* (trans. A. J. Krailsheimer; New York: Penguin, 1966), 32.

2. George R. Beasley-Murray, *A Theology of the Book of Revelation* (Cambridge: Cambridge University Press, 1993), 151.

3. I owe this to William Barclay, *The Beatitudes and the Lord's Prayer for Everyman* (New York: Harper & Row, 1963).

4. Helmut Thielicke, *The Prayer that Spans the Word* (trans. John W. Doberstein; London: James Clarke & Co., 1960), 14.

5. Jan Milic Lochman, *The Lord's Prayer* (trans. Geoffrey W. Bromiley; Grand Rapids: Eerdmans, 1990), 147.

6. Ray Stedman, *Jesus Teaches on Prayer* (Waco, Texas: Word Books, 1964).

7. Dana and Mantey, *A Manual Grammar of the Greek New Testament* (Toronto: MacMillan, 1927), 174, 176.

8. F. Dale Bruner, *The Christbook: Matthew 1-12* (Waco, Texas: Word, 1987), 242.

9. D. Elton Trueblood, *The Lord's Prayers* (New York: Harper & Row, 1965), 52.

10. Ibid., 52.

11. For a helpful discussion of this see Dallas Willard, *The Divine Conspiracy* (San Fransico: HarperSanFrancisco, 1998), 66-82.

12. Howard E. Butt, *Renewing America's Soul: A Spiritual Psychology for Home, Work, and Nation* (New York: Continuum, 1996), 7.

13. "Father knows best" is the way F. Dale Bruner put it in a lecture at Whitworth College, July 1997.

14. Thielicke, *The Prayer that Spans the World*, 35.

15. N. T. Wright, *The Lord and his Prayer* (Grand Rapids: Eerdmans, 1996), 9.

CHAPTER 2: MAKE YOURSELF REAL

1. Lochman, *The Lord's Prayer*, 28.

2. Willard, *The Divine Conspiracy*, 258.

3. See H. Seebass, C. Brown, "hagios," *The New International Dictionary of New Testament Theology*, Vol. 2, ed. Colin Brown (Grand Rapids: Zondervan, 1976), 223-231 [hereafter *NIDNTT*]; and O. Procksch, K. Kuhn, "hagios", etc., *Theological Dictionary of the New Testament*, Vol. 1, ed. Gerhard Kittel (trans. Geoffrey W. Bromiley; Grand Rapids: Eerdmans, 1964), 88-114 [hereafter *TDNT*].

4. John Calvin, *Commentary on the Gospel According to St. John* (trans. T. H. L. Parker; Oliver & Boyd, 1961), p. 68 (on John 13:31) and p. 135 (on John 17:1). Quoted from John R. W. Stott, *The Cross of Christ* (Downers Grove: Ill.: InterVarsity Press, 1986), 206.

CHAPTER 3: YOUR KINGDOM COME

1. Annie Dillard, *Teaching a Stone to Talk* (New York: Harper & Row, 1982), 40.

2. See J. Jeremias, *The Prayers of Jesus* (Naperville, Ill.: Allenson, 1967), for an understanding of first-century Jewish prayers.

3. For helpful background on why the early years of the first century were "the fullness of time" see James S. Stewart, *The Life and Teachings of Jesus Christ* (Nashville: Abingdon, 1978), 15-16.

4. Mortimer Arias, *Announcing The Reign of God: Evangelization and the Subversive Memory of Jesus* (Philadelphia: Fortress Press, 1984). This is, in my view, the best work on Jesus' teaching on the Kingdom of God in the English language.

5. From George Ladd's first significant work on the Kingdom, *Jesus and the Kingdom* (Waco, Texas: Word, 1964). It was republished under the title *The Presence of the Future* (1974). For an even more complete study see his *A Theology of the New Testament*, rev. ed. (Grand Rapids: Eerdmans, 1993), 31-211.

6. George R. Beasley-Murray, *Jesus and the Kingdom of God* (Grand Rapids: Eerdmans, 1986), 73.

7. This was the significant insight of New Testament scholar C. E. B. Cranfield in *The Gospel According to St. Mark* (London: Cambridge University Press, 1959), 66-67.

8. Cranfield, *The Gospel According to St. Mark*, 66.

9. Ibid.

10. See W. Mundle, "Revelation," in *NIDNTT* 3:309-317.

11. Ibid.

CHAPTER 4: FULFILL ALL YOUR GOOD PLEASURES

1. Thielicke, *The Prayer That Spans The World*, 33.

2. See D. Muller, "boulomai" in *NIDNTT* 3:1015-1018; and G. Schrenk, "thelo, thelema" in *TDNT* 3:44-62.

3. E. Stanley Jones, *The Christ of the Mount* (Nashville: Abingdon, 1931), 14, 19, 312.

4. W. Foerster, "Exousia," *TDNT* 2:562-574

5. See my essay, "Co-Lovers" in *Experiencing the Trinity* (Vancouver, B.C.: Regent College Publishing, 2001), 57-70.

6. C. S. Lewis, *The Weight of Glory and Other Addresses* (New York: HarperCollins, 1949; 2001), 26.

CHAPTER 5: BE OUR PROVIDER

1. Lochman, *The Lord's Prayer*, 83.

2. Wright, *The Lord and his Prayer*, 38.

3. Lochman, *The Lord's Prayer*, 88.

4. Source unknown.

5. Barclay, *The Beatitudes and the Lord's Prayer for Everyman*, 220.

6. Ibid.

7. Martin Luther, *The Larger Catechism* (trans. F. Bente and W. H. Dau; St. Louis: Concordia Publishing House, 1921), 565-773.

8. Bruner, *The Christbook*, 250.

9. Mary A. Lathbury, 1877.

10. Quoted by Krister Stendahl in "Your Kingdom Come," *Cross Currents* 32/3 (1982): 263.

11. A.J. Flint, "He Giveth More Grace" (1941).

12. Willard, *The Divine Conspiracy*, 261.

CHAPTER 6: CANCEL ALL OUR DEBTS

1. See F. Hauck, "opheilo, opheilema," in *TDNT* 5:559-565.

2. William Barclay, *The Beatitudes and the Lord's Prayer for Everyman*, 227.

3. Ibid.

4. Ibid.

5. Thielicke, *The Prayer That Spans The World*, 91.

6. Origen, *On Prayer*, (trans. William A. Curtis; Grand Rapids: Christian Classics Ethereal Library) at <www.ccel.org/o/origen/prayer/prayer.htm>. See also *Origen: Selected Writings: An Exhortation to Martyrdom, Prayer, and First Principles, etc.* (trans.. Rowan Greer; New York: Paulist, 1979).

7. Ibid.

8. J.B. Phillips, *The New Testament in Modern English* (London: Geoffrey Bles, 1960).

9. Source unknown.

10. Horatio G. Spafford in his hymn, "It is Well with My Soul."

11. Barclay, 235.

12. Luther, *The Larger Catechism*.

13. I first learned this inter-connectedness from Stuart Briscoe at a Pastors' Conference at Mt. Hermon Christian Conference Center, Santa Cruz, California, January, 1978.

14. John R.W. Stott, *Christian Counter-culture: The Message of the Sermon on the Mount* (Downers Grove, Ill.: InterVarsity Press, 1978), 149.

15. Lewis Smedes, *Forgive and Forget: Healing the Hurts We Do Not Deserve* (San Francisco: Harper, 1984), 133.

CHAPTER 7: RESCUE US!

1. Daniel P. Fuller, *The Unity of the Bible* (Grand Rapids: Zondervan, 1992), 179-183.

2. Dietrich Bonhoeffer, *Creation and Temptation* (New York: Macmillan, 1959), 51.

3. John Goldingay, "The Old Testament and Christian Faith: Jesus and the Old Testament in Matthew 1-5, Part 2," *Themelios*, 8.2 (1983): 5-12.

CHAPTER 8: NOT ALL THAT COMPLICATED

1. Larry Hurtado, *At The Origins of Christian Worship* (Grand Rapids: Eerdmans, 1999), 107.

2. F. Dale Bruner, *Christbook*, 255.

3. Wright, *The Lord and his Prayer*, 81.

CPSIA information can be obtained
at www.ICGtesting.com
Printed in the USA
LVHW020250160219
607754LV00001B/19